DUTCH
HOUSES AND
CASTLES

DUTCH
HOUSES AND
CASTLES

Text by **Jorge Guillermo**
Photographs by **Nicolas Sapieha**

Introduction by
Heimerick Tromp
Adriaan W. Vliegenthart, O.B.E.

M.T. Train/Scala Books, New York
Distributed by
Rizzoli International Publications Inc.

To my Mother

We thank H.R.H. Princess Juliana of the Netherlands,
whose gracious cooperation made it possible to photograph the Royal Palace of Soestdijk.
We are indebted to Mrs. Elizabeth van Weezendonk and Mrs. Ingrid Schram de Jong,
who helped with the translation of many difficult sources
and with the general preparation of the manuscript.
We are grateful to
Mr. P. Baars, Mr. J. Barnouw, Mr and Mrs. C. van Beuningen, Mr. N.W. Conijn,
Miss Elisabeth Dolleman, Drs. A.W.H. van der Goes, Mr. G. Heuff,
Mr. A. Kraayenga, Mr. R.J.F. van Laar, Mr. M. Loonstra, Drs. W. Overmars,
Jonkheer Dr. C.C.G. Quarles van Ufford, Mr. D.J. Schulp,
Mr. F.J. Veldman, Mrs. Ria Verhoeff, and Jonkheer, R.E.W. van Weede,
all of whom lent most valuable assistance.
Our most sincere thanks go to the private owners
and the controlling foundations of all the houses included in this volume
without whose kind involvement this project would not have been possible.

Project directed by
M.T. Train
Design and production
B2 Atelier de Design:
José Brandão / Nuno Vale Cardoso

Photo credits:
All photographs by *Nicolas Sapieha* except the following:
F. Venturi-Kea Publishing, pages: 54, 55, 56, 70, 71, 86, 87, 88, 89, 100 top,
101, 105, 109, 146, 147, 186, 187
Courtesy of *Rijksmuseum Paleis Het Loo:* pages 94, 95, 96, 97, 99
RVD: pages 110, 169
Capital Press: pages 163, 165, 167

Colour separation by Grafiseis, Amadora
Photosetting by Textype, Lisbon
Printed by Printer Portuguesa, Mem Martins

Copyright © 1990, M.T. Train-Scala Books, New York
Photographs © 1990, Nicolas Sapieha

Published by M.T. Train / Scala Books, New York
Distributed in the United States and Canada by
RIZZOLI INTERNATIONAL PUBLICATIONS INC.
300 Park Av. South, New York N.Y. 10010

Available in the Netherlands from
SDU, THE HAGUE
Available in the United Kingdom from
TAURIS PARKE BOOKS, LONDON

ISBN 0 935748 94 6
LC 90-060775

Depósito legal 39 990/90

The Netherlands

1

● Leeuwarden   ● Groningen

2

● Assen

● Lelystad   ● Zwolle
5

4   6

Harlem ●   Amsterdam ●   7
26   25

17   3
16
18   15   10
8
27   11   9
28   Utrecht ● 19   13   12
● The Hague   20
29   21   Arnhem ● 14
● Rotterdam   22   24
23

30

● Den Bosch
32

33

31 ● Middelburg

34

● Maastricht
36   35

The purpose of this map is only to indicate the approximate location of the houses and castles in this book.

Contents

Introduction

The Dutch Country House, a Bird's-Eye View.

Dutch country houses and castles, as well as their gardens and landscapes, have recently begun to attract increasing interest. Thus far, however, the study of their histories and interrelationships remains fragmentary; there is no comprehensive work dealing with their respective architects, builders, residents, and development over time.

The various houses chosen for this book offer a brief overview of the development of Dutch domestic architecture over the centuries. The buildings described range from fortified structures designed solely for military purposes to pleasant country houses set amid scenic surroundings. Upon viewing these historic buildings and their settings, one may ask what distinguishes them from their counterparts in other countries. The Irish historian W.E.H. Lecky, when visiting The Netherlands in 1873, made a comparison with England: "The houses struck him as more human institutions, much better both for the owners and for the Country than most English ones, being a smaller scale, without the vast lawns and parks... At the same time he found they had a great deal of finished and concentrated beauty, magnificent trees, beautiful lakes and extremely fine gardens and hothouses; sometimes very fine pictures; and there was a wonderful air of comfort about it all." With his remark about the smaller scale he touched on the core of one of the most striking characteristics of the Dutch country houses. Another one is the use of brick, often in combination with stone for the contrasting decorative elements. Only in the province of Limburg, where quarries can be found, is stone used more extensively, but even here the basic structural elements are mainly of brick. Compactness is also typical, since house and garden or park are, as a rule, closely aligned, forming a unit that stresses the relationship between structure and setting. The latter, not surprisingly, often includes water. In particular, the country houses of the western part of the country are often set on the bank of a river or canal or the shore of a lake, making them easily accessible. But the Dutch landed gentry also enjoyed the display of water for its own sake. Visitors from abroad often remarked upon the waterworks in the gardens of Het Loo Palace, and even the smallest house was likely to be surrounded by a moat or to have a fish pond in its garden. The landed gentry also took an interest in plants, flowers and trees. By the eighteenth century, the Dutch had begun to export their landscaping skills, as shown by the gardens of Schönbrunn in Austria. These were laid out for the Empress Maria Theresia by Schuurmans Stekhoven of Leiden.

The moated Muiderslot is a good example of the medieval fortress residence. Characteristic is the square plan in which the living quarters surround an inner court. This type of structure succeeded the single round tower called a donjon or keep, which was less convenient to live in. After 1250 many of these square castles appeared throughout The Netherlands. It is thought that they may have been introduced by Crusaders returning from the Holy Land, where Europeans had been building such castles for a long time. As presently appointed, Muiderslot recalls the seventeenth-century atmosphere of the Golden Age, when the famous poet Pieter Corneliszoon Hooft, the constable of Muiden, used to play host to his literary friends in this house.

Most Dutch medieval castles — such as Walenburg and Lunenburg Castle — were constructed according to a much simpler plan. These sites are near one another along the Langbroekerwetering, a canal dating from the twelfth century and built in order to drain a long, narrow stretch of marshland. The Bishop of Utrecht and the Dean of his Cathedral, who owned the land, gave pieces of it as rewards to selected individuals for important military or civil services. From 1250 onward, these landowners built their keeps here — simple rectangular towers usually two or three stories high. Only Sterkenburg, the oldest fortified house in the area, has a round tower. In the course of time, these houses were rebuilt to suit the prevailing taste, but the medieval donjon always remained central. Both Walenburg and Lunenburg were restored in the 1960s, the latter then being stripped of its nineteenth-century exterior to reveal its original character.

Our detailed knowledge of many of these buildings goes back only as far as the sixteenth century or thereabouts. For instance, Cannenburch and Twickel Castle were built during the Middle Ages, but only their moats and parts of the outside walls remain from that time. Their present shape dates from around 1550 when both castles were rebuilt in the Renaissance style. This is seen in their many classical elements, including pilasters, architraves, gables, shell-and-mask motifs. The central part of the façade at Twickel was richly decorated with images depicting the Fall of Man. Cannenburch's entrance tower incorporates portraits of the lord and lady of the castle. Cannenburch retained its medieval floor plan, but Twickel represented an altogether new type of layout designed to serve the domestic needs of its residents. Following the French fashion, and in imitation of the palaces of the Stadtholders and the high nobility, such as those in Breda and at IJsselsteyn, Twickel was subdivided into apartments.

The exterior of Keppel Castle was rebuilt in about 1600. At that time, even the name of the architect in charge, Willem van Bommel, was recorded. He first rebuilt the medieval keep, completing this in 1614, he then added the entrance tower with a new front, decorated with a large number of Renaissance elements. Many of these were drawn from the pattern books published by Cornelis Florisz and Hans Vredeman de Vries, whose influence extended to the layout of the enclosed garden. Elaborately planned around sixteen separate sections, the garden at Keppel survived well into the eighteenth century. The designs of Vredeman de Vries, who can be considered among the very first garden architects, were widely imitated throughout Europe.

Later, in the seventeenth century, in response to the classic ideals espoused by the Italian architects Andrea Palladio and Vincenzo Scamozzi, there was a reaction against the excessive use of decorative elements. A more sober architectural style appeared, as may be seen in Hofwijck near The Hague. This cube-shaped house was quickly rebuilt as a retreat from the intrigues of the court. The unusual garden is arranged in various sections corresponding to the parts of the human body: the house itself was the head, with pairs of windows forming the eyes, ears, and nostrils. Avenues formed the limbs and the bridge connecting the house to its garden stood for the heart. Contantijn Huygens, who designed Hofwijck for his own use, wrote: "the key to my heart is the key to this garden."

The Oranjezaal at Huys ten Bosch is one of the pinnacles of this period's classical style. It is a rare example of Dutch court architecture and a monument to Stadtholder Prince Frederik Hendrik, Prince of Orange. In houses such as Weldam and Heeze, Dutch classicism shows divergent tendencies. Weldam Castle derives its strong vertical accent from the corner blocks and the use of pilasters. The architect was probably Philips Vingboons, whose influence can be seen in many country houses in the province of Overijssel. At Heeze Castle the total absence of decoration accentuates the basic architecture. The present house — originally intended as a coach house of the castle which was never built — reflects the refined taste of the architect Pieter Post (1663 and following years). The style of Amerongen Castle is well in keeping with the new sobriety. Towering out of its moat like a monumental block, it must have made a magnificent impression at the time it was completed. The interior also testifies to the high rank and dignity of its inhabitants. The double staircase, built in 1677 by Ambassador Godard Adriaan van Reede, was modelled on the one at Mauritshuis in The Hague and leads to the Upper Gallery, originally used to receive official guests. This Gallery houses a large series of portraits of successive generations of lords and ladies of Amerongen which is unique in The Netherlands.

Since its restoration, the Het Loo Palace — built 1685-1692, restored 1977-1984 — offers an excellent example of the typical Dutch unity between house, garden, and interior which we only knew from prints and bird's eye views. The Huguenot architect Daniel Marot was responsible for the decoration of the interior as well as for the design of the garden. The Long Gallery, which had been demolished to make room for later additions, has been rebuilt, and the series of grand State Rooms planned by Marot for the King-Stadtholder William III and his wife, Queen Mary II, have been returned to their original splendour. Overall, Het Loo Palace offers a clear impression of the House of Orange's seventeenth-century domestic environment.

In the first half of the eighteenth century, Daniel Marot and his son Jacob worked for many members of the gentry and nobility; for instance, for Arnold Joost van Keppel, Daniel designed De Voorst where only the outer walls still remain. At Duivenvoorde Castle, he probably designed the decoration of the Great Room for the Van Wassenaer family, while Jacob designed the entrance to Slot Zuylen for the Van Tuylls. He made the original medieval house more livable by adding a central hall and staircase.

Throughout the ages, it was especially the entrance gate and main façade that reflected the owners' wish to follow the prevailing architectural fashion coming mainly from France. The Huis te Manpad has an elaborate gateway, with stone pillars topped with ornamental vases in Louis XIV style. The French influence is especially notable in the interior, in this respect Het Huys ten Donck, built in 1746, is an excellent example of a Dutch house inspired by French models. The Main Drawing Room with its panelling, reflects the Louis XV style, while the Dining Room, in the Louis XVI style, suggests the new vogue for more sober and restrained ornamentation. This house has one of the oldest landscaped parks laid out in The Netherlands. During the nineteenth century, this style was to determine the layout of gardens and parks not only around castles and country houses but also in cities and towns, where public gardens were now beginning to appear.

In about 1815, the seventeenth-century hunting lodge at Soestdijk was completely rebuilt and enlarged for the Dutch hero of Waterloo, later King Willem II. Two landscape architects, Jan David Zocher and his son, designed the large park which is now regarded as one of the best-preserved examples of its kind. In this park sits the white palace, like a classical temple in a Dutch Arcadia. The Empire appearance of Soestdijk Palace is credited to the architect Jan de Greef.

Because of the romantic associations with the age of chivalry, castles, and often country houses, easily lend themselves to the neo-Gothic style, which reached The Netherlands from England in the early nineteenth century. Later examples include De Haar Castle near Utrecht, and Mheer Castle in the province of Limburg. While in other parts of Europe architects were beginning to look elsewhere for inspiration, the architect P.J.H. Cuypers rebuilt the late-medieval De Haar for his patron Baron Etienne van Zuylen Nijevelt. In this building the history of the catholic Van Zuylen family is reflected in the light of christian chivalry. The picturesque gardens of his castle inspired the *très riches heures* of De Haar; they are seen to full advantage from one of the castle's many rooms. Other Dutch architects of this period returned to the Dutch Renaissance style, as at Epema State which was built in the late nineteenth century in the Province of Friesland. Indeed, the styles of the early seventeenth and eighteenth centuries had left their mark in Friesland long before. This tradition was perpetuated in the façade of Epema State and remains influential, not only in The Netherlands, but in places as varied as England and the United States, to the present day.

The Dutch palaces, castles and country houses are today part of the country's living patrimony. One typical example is De Wiersse, this eighteenth-century country house near Vorden was renovated, first by the great advocate of the conservation of historic monuments Victor de Stuers, then by his daughter and grandson. It is surrounded by a series of gardens which were continuously improved during the last century. De Wiersse represents one of the numerous Dutch country houses and gardens which have been successfully preserved by their owners.

Heimerick Tromp
Cultural Historian
Former Curator of
HET LOO PALACE

Adriaan W. Vliegenthart O.B.E.
Director of
HET LOO PALACE

The North

MENKEMABORG

Uithuizen, Province of Groningen

Menkemaborg owes its name to a family named Menkema, whose presence in the village of Uithuizen was first chronicled in the fourteenth century. The house is situated in the northernmost corner of the country, extremely close to the North Sea coast. Twenty kilometres to the south lies the city of Groningen, which has always been the political and commercial centre of the region.

The tranquil polder landscape of this area is punctuated today by small quiet villages and farms. In former times, however, life here was not always peaceful. During the early Middle Ages, Groningen was controlled by the Frisians, a fierce and independent people who held sway over a vast territory stretching along the North Sea from Belgium to Germany. The province later became the scene of a violent civil war between the rural and urban oligarchies.

Nothing is known about the appearance of the medieval house, but most likely it was a simple brick structure. Since the word *borg* means "fortified stronghold," it can be assumed that the house was encircled by a protective moat. A large stone built into the brickwork on the east wall of the house is carved with the inscription *Anno 1400 is Menckema Hues vornelt / Anno 1614 dorch Gots gnade gereparert / essende is de doot,* which means "Menkema House was destroyed in 1400 / by God's grace

Menkemaborg
The decoration of the main drawing room was planned at the beginning of the eighteenth century. The ornate fireplace is the work of the sculptor Jan de Rijk. The walnut cabinet opens to reveal an organ.

16

repaired in 1614/living is the dead.'' The local archives record that many strongholds in this part of Groningen were destroyed around 1400, during the ongoing conflict between the city and its surroundings. It is unlikely that the destruction of the Menkemaborg was as total as the inscription suggests. The house is known to have been inhabited during the fifteenth and sixteenth centuries. The 1614 rebuilding was carried out by Osebrandt Clant, whose ancestors had been living there since 1489.

A much clearer idea can be formed of the appearance of the house during Clant's time, since all the walls from 1614 have been preserved. The house then was three times larger than the older structure and was built around an open courtyard. The entrance was on the east side, which is where the inscribed stone was logically placed.

In 1682, the Menkemaborg was bought by Mello Alberda. His son, Unico Allard Alberda, inherited the property in 1699 and engaged a local architect, Allert Meijer, to remodel the house. A block of rooms was fitted into the place formerly occupied by the courtyard, and a new entrance front with a shallow forecourt was created on the north side.

Meijer made no attempt to disguise the breaks between the separate parts that became a single dwelling. From the east and west, the Menkemaborg resembles a group of three canal houses, joined but distinct. The central section rises higher than the other two, with step gables decorating the north part. Meijer purposely kept the exterior of the house modest and unpretentious. Throughout this book, the reader will find other examples of this quintessentially Dutch penchant for maintaining a low profile.

The Menkemaborg is approached from the north. Ornamental turrets stand in the corners of the small forecourt. Above the entrance door are the coats of arms of Unico Allard Alberda and his wife, Everdina van Berum. The plain exterior does not hint at the exuberance within. The entrance leads directly into a central hall, three metres wide and almost 20 metres long, built at the end of the eighteenth century to run the full depth of the house.

The decoration of most of the rooms that open onto this central hall was planned by Meijer between 1701 and 1705. Based on his designs, the sculptor Jan de Rijk carved five remarkable fireplace surrounds, four of which are still in the house. The largest and most elaborate of these was placed in the main drawing room. Richly ornamented with a profusion of flowers, birds, and human figures, this is a very important example of Dutch eighteenth-century wood carving. Set directly below a segmental pediment is an oval mythological scene painted by the Frisian artist Herman Collenius.

The gentlemen's study occupies the northeast corner of the house. Ingeniously concealed behind the sumptuous wallpaper is a large pantry. Illusionistic paintings entirely cover the inside of this secret alcove. The walls, ceiling, and even the inner surface of the doors have been decorated with classical scenes. A collection of Chinese porcelain, dating mostly from the Kangxi period, is displayed in the room.

The visitor arrives in the oldest part of the house at the south end of the central corridor. A flight of steps leads to the state bedroom, built over the old kitchen. When King William III of the Netherlands visited the Menkemaborg in 1873, he probably slept in this room. The bed, upholstered in yellow silk, was ordered for the house in 1710. The design was inspired by the work of Daniel Marot, who was the most influential architect in the Netherlands at that time.

The last private resident of the Menkemaborg was Gerhard Alberda van Menkema en Dijksterhuis, whose family presented the property to the Province of Groningen in 1921. Five years later, the Menkemaborg was opened to the public as a museum. It attracts thousands of visitors every year.

Menkemaborg
The engraved designs of Daniel Marot helped create a fashion for elaborate state beds in the Netherlands. In 1710, when the one at the Menkemaborg was ordered, it must have been the most expensive piece of furniture in the house. Such beds were seen as symbols of wealth and social position. They were also extremely practical, as the heavy hangings kept out both noise and the cold night air.

EPEMA STATE

Ysbrechtum, Province of Friesland

Top and left:
Only the gatehouse, dated 1652,
remains from the seventeenth century
building.

Bottom:
Although designed in the style of the
Dutch Renaissance, the façade of
Epema State was built at the end of
the nineteenth century to support an
earlier wall that was in danger of
collapsing.

The Frisians, who occupy the area immediately north of the former Zuider Zee, have always been an autonomous people. In the fifteenth century, when the Netherlands passed to the Duke of Burgundy, only the Frisians refused to recognize his authority. Their independent ways remained unchanged even after 1523, when the region was finally subjugated by the Emperor Charles V. The Frisians appointed their Stadholders from the Frisian branch of the Nassaus. In 1702, a Frisian prince, Johan Willem Friso, became Prince of Orange. He is a direct ancestor of every European monarch reigning today.

Like the Scots, the Frisians have always maintained their own identity. Their language, which is still widely spoken in the province, bears a close resemblance to English. The Frisian word *state* means "landed property" or "estate." Since many of the earliest recorded owners of Epema were called Epe or Epa, among other variants, the name of the property can be said to mean "estate of those called Epe."

A farm on this site was first recorded in the fifteenth century. It passed

Epema State
The kitchen holds a fine collection of traditional painted furniture from Hindeloopen, a neighbouring fishing village on the former Zuider Zee.

through an extraordinary number of different owners before 1651, when it was bought for 13,520 guilders by Duco Martena van Burmania, a Frisian aristocrat. By 1723, when the first known drawing of the house was made, it had been turned into a large, sprawling mansion. Only the gatehouse still remains from those days. Every other feature of the house was repeatedly altered during the eighteenth and nineteenth centuries. In 1878, an enormous tower was added on the roof, which caused serious structural problems and later had to be removed. The front of the house needed to be reinforced by a supporting wall.

The approach to the house leads through the gatehouse, dated 1652. The dominant feature of the main façade is the step gable placed directly over the entrance portal. The sober decoration of the central corridor includes some fine ancestral portraits. The main living areas of the house

Epema State
The large fireplace in the dining room is almost completely covered with tiles. A series of portraits of various generations of the house's owners decorate the room.

are built along the southeast wall to maximise the light.

The front sitting room contains an important set of English mahogany chairs and an engaging portrait by the nineteenth-century artist Christoffel Bisschop of Baroness Catharina van Welderen Rengers wearing Frisian costume. The decoration of the back sitting room centres on the fireplace, built around an old replica of a Titian painting now in the collection of Lord Elgin. The charming and evocative interiors of Epema State can be viewed by visitors during the summer months. The house remains the property of Maria Clara van Eysinga, born Baroness van Harinxma thoe Slooten, a descendant of the many Burmanias and Rengers who have lived here since 1651.

The East

KASTEEL CANNENBURCH

Vaassen, Province of Gelderland

The castle of Cannenburch and its park lie on the eastern edge of the Veluwe, an area of Gelderland noted for its forests and heaths. A fortified house is known to have stood on this spot as early as 1365, and, starting in 1402, it became a fief of the Dukes of Gelderland. By the following century, however, it had fallen into ruin. In 1543, the property was acquired by Marten van Rossem, a commander in the service of the Duke of Gelderland, who transformed what remained of the medieval house into a residence fit for a important courtier.

Using the original foundations and whatever walls were still standing, Van Rossem built a graceful brick castle with square corner blocks flanking a slightly higher central tower. In 1555, when Van Rossem died, construction of the new house had not been finished. Work was completed by Hendrik van Isendoorn à Blois, a distant nephew of

Left:
The appearance of Cannenburch in the middle of the seventeenth century was recorded in a large painting showing the family trees of Elbert van Isendoorn Blois and his wife, Maria van Essen, who lived in the house.

Right:
The main façade has not been changed since 1751, when the entrance was moved away from the central tower.

27

Cannenburch.

Left:
Extremely rare examples of seventeenth-century Dutch chairs with their original upholstery are kept in the state bedroom.

Top left:
The family portraits in the entrance hall have been there since the middle of the eighteenth century.

One of the series of ten horse paintings that hang in the dining room. They were probably commissioned to record the different breeds in Prince William V's stables.

Van Rossem, who inherited the property in 1563. Carved stone portraits of Hendrik and his wife can be seen on the entrance front above their coats of arms.

The Van Isendoorns continued to live at Cannenburch for three centuries. Hendrik's grandson, Elbert, enlarged the house between 1661 and 1664, and, as a result, the symmetry of the original design was lost. Fortunately for us, the aspect of the earlier house had been preserved in a painting, now displayed in the upstairs hall, done at the time of Elbert's marriage in 1645. Elbert's grandson, Frederik Johan van Isendoorn à Blois, was the last to make major alterations to the house. He changed the main entrance from the central tower to the side, constructed a stone terrace in front, and built a bridge leading to it. "*Renovatum 1751*" was carved above the new entrance door.

Cannenburch.
Portraits of the young Prince William V of Orange and his sister, Princess Carolina, flank the concealed buffet in the dining room.

Oppposite page:
This extraordinary cabinet incorporating Chinese panels inlaid with soapstone carvings is one of the most luxurious examples of Dutch furniture from the William and Mary period.

Cannenburch has remained in this form until the present. The last of the Van Isendoorns, Frederik Karel Theodoor, who served as chamberlain under three Dutch kings, died childless in 1865. In 1881, after the death of his widow, the house came under threat of demolition, but in the end, stripped of all its contents, it was sold to Baron Eduard van Lynden. The last private owner was Richard Cleve, a painter from Berlin, from whose widow the house passed to the State of the Netherlands. In 1951, the Foundation of Friends of Castles in Gelderland bought Cannenburch for the token sum of one guilder. The castle was completely restored between 1975 and 1981, and many paintings and important pieces of furniture which had been dispersed were successfully traced and brought back to the house.

Cannenburch is approached from the south. Symmetrical coach houses flank the open forecourt, which is separated from the house by a moat. The entrance front is dominated by its tower, which projects forward and is topped by an onion dome. Superimposed on the brick is an elaborate arrangement of architectural elements in carved stone, placed here by the anonymous architect for their decorative effect. The use of such ornament was quite novel in this part of the country in the sixteenth century, and indicates that Van Rossem was eager to build a fashionable house.

The carved oak panelling in the large entrance hall was installed in the middle of the eighteenth century for Frederik Johan van Isendoorn à Blois and his wife, Countess Anna van Renesse. Portraits of this couple and their respective ancestors decorate the walls. The patterned floor is laid with tiles in white marble and red Swedish stone. The two elaborately carved and gilded tables were part of the original inventory

Cannenburch.
Right and left.
Cannenburch's chapel is a great rarity
for a Dutch country house.
The Van Isendoorns, owners of the
house for many generations, were
Roman Catholics.

of the house. West of the entrance hall is the state bedroom, which contains part of a set of William and Mary chairs made for the house to designs of Daniel Marot. Amazingly, they retain their original late seventeenth century upholstery.

An extensive blue-and-white Chinese export porcelain dinner service, originally the property of the Van Isendoorns and dating from the eighteenth century, is displayed in the dining room. The walls, covered in soft green damask, are hung with a charming series of ten horse paintings by Tethart Philip Christiaan Haag, court painter of Prince William V of Orange. They probably represent the different breeds found in the princely stables in The Hague. The ceiling in this room, rediscovered at the time of the recent restoration, is painted with a design of birds and clouds and dates from the seventeenth century.

Cannenburch is open to the public throughout the year.

KASTEEL VOSBERGEN

Heerde, Province of Gelderland

The entrance façade of Vosbergen. The copper beech was planted in the beginning of the eighteenth century.

Following page, 36:
The house rises directly out of its wide moat.

Following page, 37:
Ancestral portraits and early Dutch furniture decorate the sitting room.

Vosbergen lies in the northeastern corner of Gelderland, almost on the border with Overijssel. Less than 30 kilometres to the north, at the point where the river Ijssel empties into the former Zuider Zee, is Kampen, an ancient member of the Hanseatic League and a very important trading centre during the Middle Ages. At the time of the restoration of Vosbergen, undertaken between 1972 and 1974, it was found that parts of the house may date from the fifteenth century. By 1507, it is known to have been the property of Peter Doys. His son mentioned Vosbergen in his will, written in 1558.

At the end of the sixteenth century, during the Dutch war against the Spanish, the area around Vosbergen was the site of continual action. A quieter period followed, and the house was enlarged in stages. It was probably Gerrit Krijt, a descendant of Peter Doys, who gave Vosbergen its present form. A map of 1628 identifies it as the "house of Krijt." The estate prospered during the boom years of the seventeenth century, and the Krijts acquired two mills for the manufacture of paper. By the early eighteenth century, however, the family had run into financial difficulties and Vosbergen was sold.

The magnificent copper beech in front of the house, thought to be the oldest in the country, was planted by Alexander van Dedem soon after he bought Vosbergen for 16,800 guilders in 1715. A drawing of the house done in 1730 shows the beech already in place. Very little about Vosbergen has changed since that time. The shallow rectangular forecourt is still reached by a wooden bridge, and the quiet brick façade, dated 1623, remains unadorned except by the two step gables that surmount it.

The broad expanse of the unusually wide moat makes Vosbergen appear to float on the water. No attempt has been made to conceal the seams between the various sections that make up the structure. Even inside, separate rooms have different ground levels, depending on the period of their construction.

Vosbergen is entered through the dining room, decorated in the eighteenth century. The two walls of large windows make the room very pleasantly bright. Almost one entire side of the sitting room, which is found in the eastern end of the house, is taken up by a large fireplace. The room has some early furniture and is otherwise decorated with a group of family portraits. Vosbergen is surrounded by a spacious park. The house is not open to the public.

35

KASTEEL HET NIJENHUIS

Wijhe, Province of Overijssel

Left:
A pair of extraordinary painted and gilded side chairs are displayed in the entrance hall. The walls are set with niches containing part of the collection of sculpture.

Bottom:
The entrance façade of the castle.

Kasteel Het Nijenhuis is located between the villages of Heino and Wijhe in an unspoiled rural area dotted with small farms and forests. Fifteen kilometres to the northeast is Zwolle, the capital of the Province of Overijssel.

A moated castle on this spot was mentioned as early as 1457, when Het Nijenhuis was granted to Evert van Wijtmen. His daughter, who was married to Robert van Ittersum, inherited the property in 1487. The Van Ittersums occupied the house for two hundred years, until the end of the seventeenth century. The last Van Ittersum owner, also named Robert, was a friend of William III and had fought with the King's forces against the French. Starting in 1680, he enlarged and redecorated the medieval building, possibly following the advice of Daniel Marot.

Nijenhuis.
The collection of twentieth-century art is displayed in the coach houses.

Previous pages, 40 and 41:
The walls of the main room are hung with a number of important paintings. The furniture, mostly Dutch, all dates from the seventeenth century. The exceptional grouping of Renaissance bronzes includes a portrait bust of a Spanish prelate by Gianlorenzo Bernini.

Het Nijenhuis was sold various times during the eighteenth and nineteenth centuries, and it remained unused and empty for long stretches of time. In 1840, a local newspaper carried the notice that rooms in the house could be rented from the gardener for summer parties and family receptions, and that tea, wine and a cold buffet were available. This surely must be one of the earliest public tearooms recorded in a historic building. In 1851, the property was sold to Baron van Knobelsdorff, who added two corner towers on the back of the house. Fortunately, the quiet classicism of the entrance façade was left undisturbed.

The castle is approached from the north. The layout of a moated main building with two long coach houses flanking an open forecourt is characteristically Dutch. The central section of the entrance façade is topped with a balustrade and surmounted by a gable set with a clock. The two corner wings extend forward and create a small paved terrace directly in front of the entrance door.

After passing to numerous other owners, Het Nijenhuis became the property of the Province of Overijssel. In 1958, following a complete restoration, the building was turned over to Dr. Dirk Hannema, and Het Nijenhuis entered the most interesting period of its history. In 1921, Dr. Hannema had become the director of the Boymans Museum in Rotterdam at the remarkably early age of 26. Directly before World War II, he acquired for the museum *The Supper at Emmaus*, supposedly an early work by the Dutch painter Johannes Vermeer. Considering that there are only about thirty known paintings by Vermeer, the finding and acquisition of this previously unknown masterpiece was heralded as a great

Nijenhuis.
The tower sitting room is decorated with furniture and paintings representative of the Dutch movement known as De Stijl. The three increasingly abstract studies of a tree were done by Bart van der Leck, a contemporary of Mondriaan and one of the founders of the movement in 1917.

coup. The painting was admired by all the critics and Dr. Hannema was confirmed as a major figure in the world of Dutch art.

After the war, another painting attributed to Vermeer was found in the collection of the Nazi Marshall, Hermann Göring. It was discovered that the painting had been sold to him by a Dutchman during the war. The trail led to a minor Dutch painter, Han van Meegeren, who was consequently charged with collaborating with the enemy. Van Meegeren's defense was to claim that the painting sold to Göring had not been a Vermeer, but a fake which he had painted himself. He also claimed that he had painted *The Supper at Emmaus*. The art world was taken by storm.

To prove his claim, Van Meegeren was asked to paint one more picture in the style of Vermeer. In 1947, following a sensational trial, he was found guilty of forgery, but acquitted of the more serious charge of collaboration. He was sent to jail for one year, but died before starting to serve his sentence. By then, Dr. Hannema had retired from the museum to dedicate full time to his private collection. The authenticity of *The Supper at Emmaus* remains unclear. It still hangs in the museum in Rotterdam, but without a label.

The extraordinary assemblage of paintings, sculpture, furniture and works of art acquired by Dr. Hannema over many years and now displayed in Het Nijenhuis is generally considered to be the finest Dutch private collection of its time. Dr. Hannema collected not only old masters, but also the works of contemporary artists. His modern paintings and sculptures are displayed in the coach houses. The main building holds the collection of earlier works of art.

A pair of extraordinary painted and gilded side chairs, dating from the late seventeenth century and thought to have been designed by Daniel Marot, are displayed in the entrance hall. Six identical chairs are in the Palace of Het Loo, but they have been stripped of their original paint. The walls in the entrance hall are set with niches containing part of the collection of sculpture.

The walls of the main room are covered in red silk damask and hung with a number of important paintings, including Bernardo Strozzi's *Christ and the Samaritan Woman*, which many experts consider to be the finest seventeenth-century Italian painting in the country. The paintings on the ceiling and over the elaborate fireplace are by Dionysius van Nijmegen, an eighteenth-century painter from Rotterdam. The furniture, mostly Dutch, all dates from the seventeenth century. The exceptional grouping of Renaissance bronzes includes a portrait bust of a Spanish prelate by Gianlorenzo Bernini.

Dr. Hannema lived at Het Nijenhuis until his death in 1984. The contents of the house are the property of a foundation started by him in memory of his parents. The modern collections at Het Nijenhuis are open to the public every day throughout the year. Permission to view the main building must be requested in advance.

KASTEEL ALMELO

Almelo, Province of Overijssel

The park of the castle is now confined by the town of Almelo. Until recently, however, nothing surrounded it except the flat open fields of Overijssel, the eastern most region of the Netherlands. A fortified house was first recorded in 1297. It was enlarged and rebuilt in 1662.

The building was drastically modernised in 1778 and again in 1883, when it acquired its present form. It suffered damage during World War II and was subsequently restored. The castle lies at the end of a tree-lined drive which approaches the house axially from the east. This beautiful avenue, more than three kilometres long, is known as the Counts' Alley after the owners of Almelo, Counts van Rechteren Limpurg.

In the Dutch manner, the two coach houses are arranged on either side of the open forecourt. A stone bridge leads to the main building, which is completely surrounded by a moat. The entrance front was moved forward at the time of the 1883 renovation. It is divided in three, with the two projecting corner sections framing the central block. A broken pediment is supported by four Ionic pilasters in stone and encloses the family coat of arms beneath a coronet. Almelo remains in private hands.

Left:
The entrance hall was enlarged and decorated in 1883, when it acquired its fine stucco ceilings. The white walls are hung with a group of family portraits.

Top:
This carved and inscribed plaque, dated 1662, was formerly placed on the main façade directly above the door.

Bottom:
The entrance front of the castle shows the sober classicism that is typical of this region.

KASTEEL TWICKEL

Delden, Province of Overijssel

Kasteel Twickel, just north of the town of Delden in the eastern part of Overijssel, is a magnificent castle of palatial proportions. During the Middle Ages, however, this site was occupied by a simple farmhouse. The successive efforts of four different families over six centuries contributed to this transformation. In 1347, the property was acquired by an emigrant from nearby Westphalia, Herman van Twickelo. There are no records of this early house, or any of the houses that might have replaced it, for a period of 200 years. Around 1530, Agnes van Twickelo married Gossen van Raesfelt and inherited the estate. The house they finished building in 1555 remains the nucleus of the grand mansion to be seen today.

The entrance façade of Kasteel Twickel has changed very little since that time. The rest of the building, on the other hand, has been

47

Twickel.
The orangerie.

Opposite page:
This Baroque fireplace was brought to Twickel in 1897 from the House Portugal in Delft. The white marble relief, dating from 1737, is the work of the Flemish sculptor Jan Pieter van Baurscheit the younger.

subjected to many alterations. In 1682, the property was inherited by Adriana Sophie van Raesfelt and her husband, Baron Jacob van Wassenaer Obdam, a member of a rich and distinguished family from the west of the country. As well as modernising some of the interiors, this couple enlarged the estate considerably.

The marriage of Maria Cornelia van Wassenaer to Baron Jacob van Heeckeren in 1831 marks the beginning of the final phase of the development of Kasteel Twickel. Their son, Baron Rodolphe van Heeckeren, inherited the property after his brother's death from typhoid fever. Understandably, the new owner devoted much effort to safeguarding the purity of Twickel's water supply. He constructed a water tower on the estate which still forms part of the municipal water system. The elaborate bathrooms installed in the house during his residence remain in perfect working order. His widow, born Countess Aldenburg Bentinck, started a foundation in 1953 to ensure the preservation and maintenance of the house and its large garden.

The lavish use of stone on Twickel's striking façade is an indication of the family's tremendous wealth in the middle of the sixteenth century. More important is the sophisticated division of the wall into three parts, centred on the entrance. The disproportionately narrow windows make the house seem higher than it really is, as does the tall brick centre gable. The doorway is set into a stone arch and flanked by tall half-columns supporting figures of Adam and Eve. Completing the narrative of the Fall of Man is the serpent, depicted in the precise centre of the wall. Directly over the door are the carved coats of arms of Gossen van Raesfelt and his wife.

Both the design and execution of the elaborate ornament suggest that the masons and possibly the architect employed at Twickel in the sixteenth century went on to work at Kasteel Cannenburch. The horizontal stone bands sandwiched between layers of brick, which form one of Twickel's most distinguishing features, do not appear on Cannenburch, but the façades of the two buildings are otherwise animated by the same vertical emphasis.

Twickel contains some very fine fireplaces, notably one that was brought here from a house in Delft which was demolished in the nineteenth century. The decorations include a fine collection of antique furniture, paintings, and important works of art, many of them acquired for the house by Baron Rodolphe. The large drawing room remains as arranged by his widow.

The library at Twickel was the unlikely location of an important discovery that caused a rewriting of a chapter in musical history. In the year 1740, a group of six concerti were brought out by Carlo Ricciotti, an Italian music publisher living in The Hague. Although the composer was not named, the concerti soon became very popular throughout Europe. They were eventually attributed to Giovanni Battista Pergolesi, an Italian composer who had died in 1736. They were universally accepted

Twickel.
Right:
Oriental lacquer panels are set into the
sides of this elegant table from the
large drawing room at Twickel. By the
late eighteenth century, when it was
made, the practice of using lacquer to
embellish furniture had been popular
in the Netherlands for more than a
century.

Left:
The library holds a famous collection
of incunabula and other early books.

as being by Pergolesi, were recorded as such, and were even included
in the composer's collected works, published in Rome in 1942.

Albert Dunning, a musicologist from the University of Utrecht,
discovered an eighteenth-century composition in the library of Twickel
which he identified as the original manuscript of the concerti. An
introduction handwritten in French clearly identified the composer as
Count Unico Wilhelm van Wassenaer, Lord of Twickel, who had been
born in the castle in 1692 and was baptised in the church at Delden.
Until this discovery, which established Van Wassenaer as a talented
composer, the library at Twickel had been famous mostly for its collection
of incunabula and early books. It remains for new scholars to find out
what other treasures it might hold.

KASTEEL WELDAM

Goor, Province of Overijssel

The earliest documents relating to the history of Kasteel Weldam are dated 1389. At that time, the castle belonged to Wolter van den Weldamme, a vassal of the Bishop of Utrecht. The estate is situated between the villages of Goor and Diepenheim in southeastern Overijssel. Deventer, a very important cultural and trading centre during the Middle Ages, is located on the banks of the river Ijssel a scant 30 kilometres to the east. The German border lies 25 kilometres in the opposite direction.

The two neighbouring castles of Weldam and Twickel have been closely linked on numerous occasions through the centuries. In 1506, both properties were owned by Johan van Twickelo, who left one to each of his two daughters. In the seventeenth century, Sophie van Raesfeldt, who had been brought up at Twickel, married the owner of Weldam, Johan Ripperda. Starting in 1644, they rebuilt the house. The plans were probably provided by Philips Vingboons, an important architect who designed many houses in Overijssel.

Sophie and Johan Ripperda's son inherited Weldam. In 1697, he added the remarkable octagonal chimneys decorated with acanthus leaves which still form one of the most prominent architectural features of the house. The symmetrical wings on the entrance façade were built at the same time. Since Weldam was unused for large parts of the eighteenth and nineteenth centuries, the house naturally fell into disrepair.

The next interesting period of building activity began in 1879, when Weldam was taken over by Count Carl Philipp Otto Bentinck and his wife, Countess Maria Cornelia van Heeckeren van Wassenaer, whose father owned Twickel. It was at this time that Weldam and its garden acquired the look they still retain today. Two large corner towers, one octagonal and the other square, were added on the north side of the house. Designed for the Bentincks by an English architect, W. Samuel Weatherly, and topped by decorative weathervanes, the towers provide a romantic backdrop to the strict classicism of the entrance façade.

The imposing entrance front of Weldam dates from the middle of the seventeenth century. It was probably designed by the architect Philips Vingboons.

Weldam.
The beech tunnel is almost 150 metres long.

Opposite page:
The garden was laid out at the end of the last century for Count and Countess Bentinck. The formal style of the seventeenth century was chosen to harmonize with the castle's architecture.

The Bentincks commissioned a Parisian garden designer and theorist, Edouard André, to create a new garden around Weldam, but the work was actually carried out by a Dutchman, the celebrated Hugo Poortman. He also worked for the Bentinck family at Middachten and at Twickel. Until 1984, when the restoration of the formal garden around the Palace of Het Loo was completed, the garden at Weldam was generally considered to be the finest reconstruction of a formal Dutch seventeenth-century garden.

The layout of the castle and grounds is characteristic of Dutch country houses. The square forecourt is enclosed on two sides by identical brick outbuildings. A tree-lined drive approaches Weldam axially from the south. The entrance gate is flanked by stone pillars capped by ornamental vases. The castle itself is completely surrounded by its moat and accessible only by way of a stone bridge.

The central section of the main façade dates from the rebuilding of 1644 and is faced in stone. Four pilasters capped by Ionic capitals separate the three bays of windows. The entrance door is surmounted by a classical pediment, and carved stone garlands animate the otherwise unornamented surface. It is evident that Philips Vingboons, if indeed he was responsible for the design, was conversant with the works of such classicist architects as Pieter Post and Jacob van Campen, who were the leading exponents of the style in the Netherlands. The two projecting corner blocks were built at the end of the seventeenth century.

Apart from some outstanding stucco ceilings dating from the seventeenth century, very few traces of earlier decorative schemes still

Weldam.
Right:
The moat is a reminder of Weldam's medieval origin.

Opposite page:
The tower sitting room has a Dutch Empire fireplace.

remain in the house. For the most part, the interior of Weldam was totally refurbished for Count and Countess Bentinck during the last two decades of the nineteenth century. Their grandson lives in the house today. He has taken responsibility for the maintenance of the magnificent garden, which can be visited by the public.

DE WIERSSE

Vorden, Province of Gelderland

It is interesting to note that ownership of De Wiersse has passed through the female line on many occasions during its history. The earliest known mention of the house occurs in a document of 1288, when the owner was Godelinde, Abbess of the Convent at Elten. By 1482, the property had passed to Gerrit van Vorden, who was succeeded by his granddaughter Maria. Her descendants continued to occupy the estate until 1678, when it was sold to Enno Matthias ten Broeck. Since that time, De Wiersse has remained in the hands of the same family.

Countess Aurelia Carolina van Limburg Stirum inherited the house in 1893, the year she married Jonkheer Victor de Stuers. He was the man responsible for the creation of the Dutch government department of Monuments, Museums and Archives. Between 1906 and 1916, the house was restored under his direction. De Wiersse next passed to his only daughter, Alice, who married an Englishman, Major William Gatacre. Their son and his family live in the house today.

The entrance front of De Wiersse was given its present form around 1920.

Bottom:
The garden pavilion.

De Wiersse.

Right:
Rare seventeenth-century tile pictures decorate the fireplace in the study of Victor de Stuers, which was reconstructed in one of the coach houses.

Left:
The painting set into the Rococo fireplace is a portrait of a doll. In 1900, Victor de Stuers commissioned Thérèse Schwartze, a famous Dutch society portraitist, to paint his daughter Alice. The little girl behaved so well during the sittings that she was offered a reward. Alice asked for a painting of her favourite doll, Wilhelmien. Both Alice and Wilhelmien's portraits are still in the house.

Only the moat remains of the original medieval house, which was rebuilt in 1651 and enlarged in the beginning of the eighteenth century. The semicircular entrance pavilion was added around 1920, as were the coach houses which once flanked the open courtyard. One of these was destroyed by the Germans during World War II, and the remaining one contains the study of Victor de Stuers, brought here from The Hague by his daughter and reconstructed with great care.

Although De Wiersse is not open to the public, the justly celebrated gardens can be visited on a number of days during the summer months.

VERWOLDE

Laren, Province of Gelderland

The garden front, showing the tower built in 1926.

Bottom:
The formal garden.

Verwolde lies in the middle of a wooded estate in the easternmost part of Gelderland, between the river Ijssel and the German border. Surrounded by a landscape of undisturbed serenity, there is nothing about the house to betray that it was once the site of violent warfare. In 1505, however, the Duke of Gelderland captured Verwolde from its owner, Derck van Keppel, whose family had occupied the castle since 1346.

At the Duke's command, Verwolde was surrounded by three deep moats and three protective walls, but these served only to enrage his enemies. In 1510, the castle was besieged by an army of 3,000 men, captured, and razed to the ground. Some rebuilding must have taken place before 1583, since in that year Spanish troops were garrisoned in the castle.

Verwolde.

Right:
A portrait of Prince William V of Orange hangs above a display cabinet in the sitting room. The Prince's architect, Philip Schonck, designed the house.

Opposite page:
The principal bedroom of Verwolde was turned into a dining room in the nineteenth century. Chinese porcelain is displayed in the rare Dutch corner cabinet.

By the eighteenth century, Verwolde was described as looking like a peasant's hut. In 1738, the house and one third of the estate were sold for 26,000 guilders to Baron Evert Jan Benjamin van Golstein, who acquired it for his daughter and her husband. Their son, Frederik Willem van der Borch, inherited the house in 1766, and six years later succeeded in buying the remaining two thirds of the estate. His next project was to build a new house, and probably through his brother, who was in the service of the Prince of Orange, he contacted Philip Willem Schonck, the Prince's architect. Architect and patron had their first meeting in 1775, and by the end of that year Schonck's final drawings were ready, along with his estimate that 480,000 bricks would be needed for the construction. The work took only nine months to complete, and by December of the following year, Frederik Willem was able to move into his new house.

Although Schonck's duties regularly brought him to Het Loo, less than 30 kilometres away, he very infrequently visited Verwolde. His written instructions were very clear, however, and Frederik Willem, assisted by a German mason called Schreuder, personally took charge of supervising the work. Schonck also designed the interior decoration,

Verwolde.
Right and opposite page:
The neoclassical stucco work in the
entrance hall, done by Girolamo
Columba, is all original.

which was carried out with some extravagance. Marble fireplaces and elegant furniture were brought from The Hague and Amsterdam. Frederik Willem's son inherited the house in 1787.

Since its completion in 1776, the only substantial change made to Verwolde has been the addition of the tower, built in 1926 for Baron Willem Henrik Emile van der Borch van Verwolde as part of a general renovation of the house. The tower destroys the quiet classicism of Schonck's design, but it must have been felt at that time that it gave the house more of the look of an ancient family seat. Schonck's main entrance front is distinguished by its quiet elegance. Of the five bays of windows, the central one is faced in sandstone and topped by a pediment ornamented with the coats of arms of the builder, Frederik Willem van der Borch, and his wife, Countess Sophia Juliana van Rechteren. The graceful entrance steps were added at the time of the 1926 renovation.

The symmetrical floor plan of the house has never been changed. The entrance hall has a plain white marble floor, but the walls are embellished with beautiful musical trophies carried out in stucco in the late 1770's by Girolamo Columba. In the northeast corner of the house is the charming Chinese room. The wallpaper is painted with Chinese

figures against a powder blue background and was delivered in 1778 by the Amsterdam painter J.H. Troost van Groenedoelen. The floorboards are painted in the same shade of blue.

The large sitting room faces south and opens onto a wide terrace, which was added to the house in 1926 to overlook the formal garden designed by Hugo Poortman. The walls are covered in a patterned wallpaper and hung with family portraits. The gray marble fireplace is original, as are the overdoor paintings. A display cabinet contains an eighteenth-century Chinese export *famille rose* service which has always been in the house.

It is interesting to note that the original plan of Verwolde did not include a dining room. What is now called the dining room was initially used as the main bedroom of the house. It was turned into the dining room much later, after it had become customary to set a room aside for this purpose. The walls are covered in a golden brown *Velours d'Utrecht*. A rare Dutch eighteenth-century corner cabinet is ornamented with carved and gilt wood curtains and tassels and is filled with antique Chinese blue-and-white porcelain. The table is set with plates from the same service and surrounded by Dutch chairs dating from the 1760's. The eighteenth-century crystal chandelier is most probably English.

The library is not found on the *piano nobile* but upstairs, surrounded by the family bedrooms. This strikes the modern visitor as an unusual arrangement. At the end of the eighteenth century, however, this room was probably meant as a quiet retreat where the family could receive their closest friends. The fireplace and the wood panelling are original, although the latter was altered at the time of the 1926 renovation. The fine collection of books includes the family archives. Two iron bullets, supposedly dating from the siege of 1510, serve as reminders of Verwolde's eventful history.

The last private owner of the house was Baron Allard Philip van der Borch van Verwolde, who sold the house in 1977 to the Foundation of Friends of Castles in Gelderland. Following a period of restoration, the house was opened to the public in 1982.

DE VOORST

Eefde, Province of Gelderland

At the time of its completion in 1697, De Voorst must have been the most fashionable and luxurious private residence in the country. Given to Arnold Joost van Keppel, first Earl of Albemarle, by his great friend and patron William III, no expense was spared in the construction and decoration of the house. The designs were made by Daniel Marot and Jacob Roman, the same team who had built Het Loo for William III. Part of the large porcelain collection of Queen Mary, which had been a gift to Keppel from the King after the Queen's death, had been brought from England and was kept at De Voorst.

Just as Het Loo, the house has a higher central block joined to the lower side wings by semicircular colonnades. The construction, however, is entirely in stone, which must have been considered a great extravagance at that time. The forecourt is reached through a superb wrought iron gate capped by four potted trees with gilded oranges. This is a replica installed at the end of the nineteenth century, the original now being at the Rijksmuseum in Amsterdam. De Voorst was bought by Hendrik Völcker van Soelen in 1875 and lovingly restored by him at great expense. The house was consumed by fire in 1943, and only the outside walls were left when the Foundation of Friends of Castles in Gelderland took over the ownership. No attempt was made to restore the interiors, but at least the house was saved. Its graceful façade, evocative of a splendid past, can be seen from the highway.

Left:
De Voorst is one of the few Dutch houses constructed entirely in stone.

Bottom:
An ornamental moat surrounds the house and its garden.

The monumental fireplace in the great hall was designed around a portrait of Adriaan Werner van Pallandt surrounded by the coats of arms of five generations of his ancestors.

KASTEEL KEPPEL

Laag Keppel, Province of Gelderland

The castle assumed its present form in the early years of the seventeenth century.

Kasteel Keppel is located very close to the German border directly on the Old Ijssel, which today is an unimportant stream, but in the Middle Ages was an active waterway. The earliest known reference to Keppel occurs in a document of 1272. The castle changed hands repeatedly before 1530, when the eldest daughter of the house married Johan van Pallandt. Keppel has remained in the same family since that time.

Van Pallandt was in the service of the King of Spain. In 1582, his son, Frederik, allowed a group of Spanish soldiers to stay at Keppel. The response of the Dutch troops, who were then fighting a fierce war of independence against Spain, was to capture the castle and burn it to the ground. In 1605, Johan van Pallandt, Frederik's son, appealed to the King of Spain to compensate him for the destruction of his house. The King's answer, if any, has not been preserved.

Starting in 1612, the reconstruction of the castle was begun under the supervision of Willem van Bommel, a mason. The entrance front, crowned by an elaborate ornamental gable, was designed by him and is dated 1615. Late in the next century, the entrance hall was redecorated in the neoclassical style with graceful stucco trophies representing the fine arts. These were done by Giuseppe Peretti, an itinerant Italian craftsman known to have started working at Keppel in 1781.

The staircase leads directly to the great hall, the largest and most impressive room in the house. It is dominated by a monumental carved-wood chimneypiece painted two shades of pink and decorated with a Japanese Imari *garniture de cheminée*. The capitals of the Corinthian pilasters and the luxuriant decoration are highlighted in white. A portrait of Adriaan Werner van Pallandt, who lived at Keppel, can be dated around 1675, the year he was confirmed Baron. It is surrounded by the coats of arms of 62 of his ancestors, two of the original 64 having been stolen during World War II.

Keppel is the property of a private foundation. Permission to visit the house must be requested in writing.

Keppel.
Only one of the original pair of coach houses survives.

74

KASTEEL MIDDACHTEN

De Steeg, Province of Gelderland.

The estate of Middachten is located along the ancient road between Arnhem on the river Rhine and Zutphen on the river Ijssel, both important cities in the province of Gelderland. Close to the Ijssel yet far enough away to be safe from flooding, the estate is excellently situated. In a country where, until this century, land routes were impassable most of the year, Middachten's proximity to the river was an essential factor in its development. Down the Ijssel was the Zuider Zee and access to Amsterdam. In the other direction lay the Rhine and passage to both Germany and the great ports on the North Sea.

The Dutch province of Gelderland was an independent duchy until the sixteenth century. It takes its name from its former capital, Geldern, a city which is now part of Germany. An improbable but endearing legend derives the name of Geldern from the exploits of a tenth-century knight called Wichard de Pont. Engaging a ferocious dragon in battle, he succeeded in inflicting a fatal wound and is said to have heard the word "gelre" repeated by the dragon as it lay dying. This so impressed the knight that when he founded a new city he named it Gelre, a name that eventually became Geldern.

Perhaps because it was named after a dying dragon's last word, Gelderland and its feudal lords engaged in frequent warfare over the ensuing centuries, a fact that naturally influenced the design of a house like Middachten. The wide moat that still surrounds the house and its outbuildings was, in earlier times, its most important defensive feature. The outbuildings, which also remain standing, at one point housed both workmen and animals. The castle sat beyond one further bridge, as it still does, in the widest part of the moat.

The estate and its manor house were first mentioned in the year 1190, when they were listed as being the property of one Jacobus de Mithdac. In 1666, the heiress of Middachten married Godard van Reede, a friend and companion of Prince William III. When William was called to England to take over the throne, Van Reede went along. He proved himself an able soldier, and eventually became commander-in-chief of the King's forces. William rewarded Van Reede by creating him Baron Aughrim and Earl of Athlone, these being the sites of two of his greatest victories in Ireland.

Although Middachten had been improved and enlarged over the years to reflect the growing political and financial importance of its owners, the fundamental layout of the medieval manor remained unchanged until the end of the seventeenth century. It was then that King Louis XIV of France invaded the Netherlands. In 1673, retreating French soldiers looted and ransacked the house. Minor repairs must have been carried out, but it was only after his return from England that Van Reede's thoughts turned to renovating the house to suit his new station.

Kasteel Amerongen, another property of Van Reede, had been rebuilt by his father after being very heavily damaged by the French, and it was available for his use. But perhaps Van Reede felt that Middachten, because of its proximity to William III's palace at Het Loo, was a better location for an ambitious courtier. Whatever his reasons, Van Reede spared no effort in his rebuilding programme. Jacob Roman, the King's architect, was engaged to provide the new designs. Roman submitted a wooden model in 1693, and supervised the demolition of parts of the old house. However, by the time construction started, in 1695, his place had been taken by another architect, Steven Vennekool, perhaps to allow Roman to devote his full attention to the King's projects. Between 1695 and 1697, the simple manor house was transformed into a grand Baroque building.

Middachten is built of red brick in the shape of an almost perfect cube. It has a square floor plan, and its height, from the water, is almost the same as its width. The flatness of the four fronts is broken by central projecting bays, the one on the main façade being faced in stone and decorated with carved military trophies. The use of stone, always a great extravagance in a country that has no quarries, gives the façade a heightened sense of grandeur. The main door has a rounded top and is flanked by tall windows, an arrangement that was evidently meant to suggest a triumphal arch. At the very top are the coats of arms of Godard van Reede and his wife, plus his motto *Malo mori quam foedari*, which means roughly "Death before disgrace."

The square vestibule has large windows set in three of its walls, and the light that they let in is extraordinarily bright. Reflections from the

Midddachten.
Statues set in niches greet the visitor upon entering the vestibule.

moat increase the brightness and dapple the whitewashed walls. From this point of entrance on, the architecture controls the visitor's perception of the interior space. As one moves out of the vestibule's deliberate brightness and into the penumbra of the central hall directly behind it, one's eyes take a few moments to adjust.

Exactly as must have happened countless times over the past three centuries and precisely as the architect intended, Middachten's splendid central hall unfolds with almost theatrical control. A double staircase now comes into view, set very cleverly into the area that had been occupied by the courtyard of the medieval house. The entire space is surmounted by an oval dome decorated with plasterwork of dazzling virtuosity, and it is here that one's attention is drawn. Putti, masks and military trophies, all designed to remind the viewer of Godard van Reede's military exploits, emerge slowly out of the soft shadows, the sunlight highlighting an occasional detail and bringing it into focus against the muted background. The names of Van Reede's great victories are inscribed on the cornice below.

The central double staircase at Middachten is undeniably one of the great architectural creations of the Dutch seventeenth century and, as

Midddachten.

Opposite page:
The central staircase of Middachten is one of the great masterpieces of Dutch domestic architecture.

Rigth:
Three details of the dome.

Following pages, 82 and 83:
The salon has large windows to let in the sunlight, always a desirable commodity in the Netherlands.

such, must be ranked among the most important achievements of Baroque domestic architecture in northern Europe. The sophisticated manipulation of light owes a great deal to the work of Bernini and makes it clear that the architects must have been familiar with the principles of the Roman Baroque.

Although the structure of the house remains as it was at the end of the seventeenth century, the decoration of the rooms reflects the many changes that occur when a building is lived in and cared for by a family for many generations. The large salon, for example, was used as a family sitting room in the early nineteenth century. During a later redecoration, an attempt was made to furnish it in an earlier style, and it is in this form that we see the room today. The walls are covered in a soft red damask and are hung with a series of portraits, including a large one of the King-Stadholder William III. A set of Louis XV giltwood arm chairs form part of the collection of fine furniture that fills the room.

Middachten is one of those rare houses that have never been sold. The present owner is Countess Ortenburg, born Countess Aldenburg Bentinck, who is a direct descendant of Everardus van Middachten, owner of the house until his death in 1315. For a few years, the house served as the official residence of the Queen's Governor in the Province of Gelderland, but in 1985 the Countess moved back and has since devoted much of her time to the restoration of the house and its garden. Occasionally, Countess Ortenburg makes the main rooms of Middachten available for receptions or dinners. The house can be visited on public holidays, and on other days by prior arrangement. The garden, restored in 1900 by the distinguished garden architect Hugo Poortman, is open to the public every day from mid-May until mid-September.

KASTEEL BILJOEN

Velp, Province of Gelderland

The earliest document relating to Kasteel Biljoen dates from 1076 and is preserved in the archives at Arnhem, less than 10 kilometres to the southwest. The present building was constructed by Duke Charles of Gelderland, who acquired the property in 1530. It is a massive square structure encircled by a moat. Each of the four corner towers is surmounted by a bell-shaped ribbed roof topped by an ornamental chimney. After passing through different owners, Biljoen was bought by Alexander van Spaen in 1661. The castle would have been destroyed by the French at the end of the seventeenth century had Louis XIV not chosen it as his headquarters.

Baron Johan Frederik Willem van Spaen redecorated Biljoen shortly after his return from the grand tour in 1770. The superb ballroom that he commissioned to be built directly over the main entrance is not only

The impressive mass of Kasteel Biljoen, dating from the sixteenth century, is surrounded by a moat.

The present bridge has replaced the original medieval drawbridge.

Biljoen.
The stucco decoration of the ballroom was carried out shortly after 1770. Piranesi's Roman vedute *inspired the overdoor scenes. The parquetry floor is original.*

the most important room in the house but unquestionably the finest example of neoclassical interior architecture in the Netherlands. From the meticulously kept accounts, it is known that four men laboured for two years to complete the stucco work. It seems unfair that only the name of the foreman, Hermann Bader, has been preserved.

The vaulted ceiling is covered with sharply detailed allegorical trophies. However, it is not the beautiful ceiling that makes this such a memorable room, but the remarkable series of Roman views placed between pairs of fluted pilasters over the four doors and above the rounded niches in the middle of the two long walls. Patterned after Piranesi's *vedute*, these scenes are executed with astonishing skill. The strict neoclassicism of the setting accentuates their spirited vitality. It is this combination of rigorous design with technical virtuosity that makes the ballroom at Biljoen an interior of true historical importance.

PALACE OF HET LOO

Apeldoorn, Province of Gelderland

Left:
The illusionistic paintings that line the great staircase were meant to blur the division between the house and its surrounding gardens.

The garden façade.

At the end of the seventeenth century, the Palace of Het Loo was already considered an extraordinary building by Dutchmen and foreigners alike. Het Loo was then, as it is today, the largest house in the country, as well as being the only royal palace ever built in The Netherlands. It was this monarchical connection that determined all aspects of the building and decoration of the house and its garden. To understand Het Loo, one must first understand its builder, the Stadholder-King William III.

William was brought up in unsettled times. His father had died eight days before William was born, leaving the country under the control of a republican oligarchy determined to exclude the young prince from power. In 1672, however, the country came under threat of attack by both France and England, and William was appointed captain-general

of the army. Within four months, the troops of Louis XIV had crossed the Rhine and had advanced to within twenty kilometers of Amsterdam. In the resulting panic, William was finally appointed Stadholder, and, emboldened by this triumph, he surrounded the French forces and managed to eject them from Dutch lands. It was a phenomenal victory, though the war would go on for another six years.

In 1677, William married his cousin, Princess Mary, heiress presumptive to the English throne. In 1685, her father, who as a Catholic was unpopular in England, became King James II. Three years later, the dreaded prospect of a Catholic dynasty was made certain by the birth of a son and heir to James. William was unequivocally Protestant and third in line of succession, so it was natural for the English to appeal to him for help. At the end of 1688, William crossed the English Channel with his troops, forcing James to escape to France. By the spring of the following year, William and Mary were crowned King and Queen of England.

William, who had been brought up an orphan, surrounded by political intrigue and uncertain of his own prospects, found himself lionized as the hero of Protestantism and king of a country far larger than his native land. His extensive building campaigns on both sides of the Channel must have resulted from a wish to create a concrete memorial to his achievements. Louis XIV, his great foe, had built a great palace at Versailles as an affirmation of his greatness. William III would attempt to do the same in his new house.

William acquired the estate of Het Loo in 1684. The property is located on sandy ground in the centre of Gelderland. *Loo* is an old Dutch word meaning a clearing in the forest, and it was obviously the sparse vegetation on the heath that gave the estate its name. William, who was a keen hunter, bought the land because of its great abundance of game. Walter Harris, William's doctor, has left us this account: "It is an excellent Country for Hunting, and abounds with Stags, some Roe-bucks, the Wild Boar, Foxes, Hares, and some Wolfs. It is no less excellent for Fowling, and has good store of Woodcocks, Partridges, Pheasants, etc." The estate had a moated castle dating from the fourteenth century, which is still in use by the royal family and is known as the Old Loo.

Drawings for a new house were prepared by the Académie d'Architecture in Paris, an unusual choice considering William's enmity with the French King, but nonetheless a telling one. The plans were ready by early 1685 and work on the house started soon thereafter. In view of the thoroughly Dutch look of the house, it is probable that the architect in charge of the construction, Jacob Roman, altered the French plans as he went along to suit William's more sober taste. The house was planned around a central block originally joined to the two long wings by quarter-circular colonnades. After William and Mary's ascension to the English throne, it became necessary to enlarge the house, and the colonnades were replaced by symmetrical corner pavilions. This second building phase, which took place between 1690 and 1692, also involved extensive interior decoration and the enlargement of the garden. Daniel Marot, a Huguenot who had arrived in Holland in 1685, was the designer in charge. His work at Het Loo marked the beginning of his association with William III and was important in disseminating the grand Baroque style of Louis XIV throughout Holland and England.

Het Loo.

Opposite page:
The Stadholder-King William III had two small cabinets decorated for his private use. The painting of exotic animals that now hangs over the fireplace is the work of Melchior d'Hondecoeter.

Following pages, 94 and 95:
Queen Mary's enthusiastic patronage helped popularise blue-and-white delftware in the Netherlands and later in England. Some of these objects are displayed in her private cabinet along with Chinese porcelain from the same period.

The King's library was designed by Daniel Marot. His engravings show how little the room has changed since its completion.

Het Loo.
The tapestry in the King's bedroom was woven in Brussels around 1690 following Marot's designs. Other tapestries from the same series hang in the state dining room.

Opposite page top:
The ceiling in Queen Mary's bedroom, painted directly on the wooden boards, was probably done by Gerard de Lairesse, a painter from Liège who spent most of his working life in the Netherlands.

Opposite page, bottom:
The seventeenth-century bed in Queen Mary's bedroom retains its original cut-velvet hangings. The set of silver furniture is unique in the Netherlands.

The next important change to the house took place in 1807, when King Louis Bonaparte had the exterior covered under a layer of gray plaster. This was later painted white, and Het Loo remained that colour until the recent restoration. Between 1875 and 1914, the house was made one story higher, and a large ballroom was added. Queen Wilhelmina retired to Het Loo after her abdication in 1948, and lived there until her death in 1962. Her daughter, Queen Juliana, renounced all further use of the house by the royal family. It was then decided to restore the palace to its seventeenth-century appearance and open it to the public as a museum devoted to the House of Orange and the part it has played in Dutch history. J. B. Baron van Asbeck was asked to direct the restoration, which took seven years to complete and cost eighty-four million guilders. In 1984, Het Loo was officially opened as a museum by Queen Beatrix.

Both the house and the garden are designed around a very clear central axis. Five tree-lined avenues converge in front of the large forecourt, which has a fountain in the centre. The fountain is carved in marble with the figures of four dolphins. The house is constructed entirely in brick, all of which was baked on the site. Stone was used only for the window sills and a few other structural details. The main entrance front has seven bays of windows, the middle three projecting forward and topped by a pediment ornamented with figures, including a bust of Diana, Roman goddess of the hunt. Segmental pediments with hunting trophies carved in stone decorate two of the corner pavilions. The figures are set against a contrasting brick background, a most unusual

feature. Directly below the central pediment and set above a sun clock is the date 1696.

The entrance hall leads to the grand staircase, designed by Marot, which is decorated with large illusionistic paintings. The originals had been destroyed, but, in 1899, Queen Wilhelmina commissioned the painter Willem Fabri to replace them, using as a model the engravings made by Marot himself in the early eighteenth century. They show various figures in exotic dress leaning over a balustrade. The audience room, which is the centre of the *piano nobile*, retains its original decoration by Marot. Although all the original furniture has disappeared, the wall paintings by Johannes Glauber are still in place. In a corner of the audience room is a table, covered with numerous mementos of the Dutch resistance movement during World War II, which were placed here by Queen Wilhelmina herself.

Arranged on either side of the audience room are the private apartments of William and Mary, each consisting of a bedroom, an antechamber, a dressing room, and a small private cabinet which was out of bounds to all but the monarchs' closest friends. It is worth noting that, before the introduction of central heating, large rooms were impossible to heat adequately. Only these small private cabinets would have been comfortable in winter. Using the original inventories as a guide, William and Mary's rooms at Het Loo have been painstakingly restored.

Queen Mary's apartment is located in the eastern half of the house. The bedroom contains a very rare English seventeenth-century bed hung with magnificent Genoese velvet and a set of matching chairs. The rarest furniture in the room, however, is a set of silver furniture made in Augsburg around 1700 by Johann Bertermann. Comprising a table, mirror and two stands, this set is unique in Holland. Mary's private cabinet is located in the northeast corner of the house and has extensive views over the garden. It is furnished entirely in the style of her time and decorated with various examples of the blue-and-white delftware that she loved so much.

The walls of William's bedroom are covered in orange damask trimmed in blue, these being the colours of the House of Orange Nassau. Above the fireplace is a flower painting by Gaspar Pieter Verbruggen. Portraits of William and Mary by Jean Henri Brandon hang on either side of the bed, which is draped in blue damask and topped with orange feathers. The painted ceiling, designed by Marot, was done directly on the wooden boards. William's private cabinet is located in the northwest corner of the house and also enjoys wide views over the garden. The walls are hung with alternating panels of red and purple damask, an unusual colour combination. A painting by Arnold Houbraken hangs over the fireplace.

The state dining room is on the ground floor and looks just as it did when Marot engraved it. The marble fireplace is topped with military emblems and flanked by a pair of superb tapestries woven in Brussels around 1690. They bear the crowned coat of arms of the King and Queen surrounded by allegorical figures, and display the motto of the House of Orange, ''Je Maintiendray,'' as well as the cipher of William and Mary. An elaborate niche at one end of the room, set in the wall behind a gilded service table, is framed by a pair of fluted pilasters with gilded

Het Loo.
A remarkable delftware tulip vase is displayed in the kitchen.
Seventeenth-century tiles entirely cover the walls.

Ionic capitals. Illusionistic paintings of stone urns are set in the corners. This part of the room is separated from the actual dining area by two fluted columns joined to the side walls by gilded balustrades and topped by gilded Ionic capitals. Whereas William's chair is upholstered in red velvet, the seats of all the other chairs are covered in blue damask.

Planned along a strong central axis, the garden of Het Loo was designed as carefully as the house and was seen as an extension of it. In the late eighteenth century, the entire garden was buried and replaced with a landscaped park. However, an exact reconstruction was made possible by the availability of numerous engravings. Separate gardens for William and Mary are located on opposite sides of the house to

Het Loo.

*Top, right and opposite page:
The formal garden was planned by
Marot along a very strong central axis
leading to semicircular colonnades. It
includes numerous fountains,
ornamental statues, and intricate
parterres.*

correspond to their apartments. The most elaborate part of the garden, laid out with intricate parterres, is placed directly behind the house and is surrounded on three sides by a raised promenade. The garden is ornamented with fountains, cascades, statues, and countless vases in marble, stone, terracotta and lead.

Het Loo was built as the showpiece of a proud King. It has been turned into a monument to an entire family. A splendid repository of countless treasures, it is a unique register of a country's history. Since its opening in 1984, it has become the second most popular Dutch museum, second only to the Rijksmuseum in Amsterdam. The palace and its garden can be visited every day except Monday.

Utrecht

PALACE OF SOESTDIJK

Soestdijk, Province of Utrecht

The white dining room, decorated in the Empire style, has not been changed since its completion in 1821.

The garden front of the palace. The ornamental lake was created in the early nineteenth century when the park was landscaped.

The Royal Palace of Soestdijk and the large park that surrounds it lie in a forested area between the villages of Soest and Baarn. This is a low region, and the soft ground formerly made travelling difficult whenever it rained. In the fourteenth century, the Bishop of Soest had a raised roadway built to facilitate traffic. It was from this road, *dijk* in Dutch, that the estate took its name.

Cornelis de Graeff, burgomaster of Amsterdam, acquired the property and, in 1650, had a simple house built on it. Soestdijk passed to his son, Jacob, who joined the forces of Prince William III. It is likely that the Prince first heard about Soestdijk from Jacob de Graeff during the campaign of 1673. The Prince was a great lover of hunting, and Soestdijk, located conveniently close to Utrecht, was rich in game. In April 1674, William III bought De Graeff's house with the surrounding forest for the sum of 18,755 guilders. He enlarged the park by systematically acquiring adjoining properties. The States of Utrecht presented him with the lordships of Soest, Baarn, and Ter Eem, all bordering on Soestdijk. Queen Beatrix still counts these among her many titles.

The architect Maurits Post was asked by the Prince to enlarge the simple house at Soestdijk. Post's father, Pieter Post, had designed the Huis ten Bosch for William's grandmother, Princess Amalia. Work on the new house was started by the end of 1674 and took four years to complete. Post designed a graceful building two stories high. The waterlogged nature of the soil made it necessary to construct the house

over a cellar partially above the ground. The central section of the main façade was framed by corner blocks, each consisting of four bays of windows. A low terrace was built directly in front of the house, and broad steps led up to the entrance. The large rectangular forecourt was closed in front by a wrought iron gate joined to symmetrical corner pavilions.

The decoration of Soestdijk included many paintings especially commissioned for the house. Two large hunting trophies, which are now in the collection of the Rijksmuseum in Amsterdam, were done by Melchior d'Hondecoeter for the entrance hall of Soestdijk. In the same collection is a mythological scene, *Selene and Endymion*, painted by Gerard de Lairesse for the bedroom of Princess Mary, William III's wife. The decorative scheme of the main rooms of the house in the late seventeenth century must have been planned around such combinations of sporting paintings and mythological scenes.

Following the Prince's acquisition of Het Loo in 1684, his visits to Soestdijk became less and less frequent. After his death in 1702, his successors continued to use the house. In 1795, along with all the other possessions of the House of Orange, Soestdijk was made the property of the Dutch nation.

At the time of the Napoleonic wars, the Prince of Orange, who would later become King William II, was Commander-in-Chief of the Dutch forces fighting against the French. He was wounded at Waterloo and became a great hero. In 1815, Soestdijk was offered to him by a grateful country. A complete renovation of the house was entrusted to a Dutch architect trained in Paris, Jan de Greef. Work started without delay and went on until 1821. The prince and his young wife, Anna Paulowna, who was the daughter of the Russian Czar, supervised the new decoration. The seventeenth-century hunting lodge was metamorphosed into a vast palace in the Empire style.

The entrance hall has a white marble floor. Large portraits of King William II and Queen Anna by François Joseph Kinson, a painter from Bruges, hang behind a pair of Empire sofas. The two white marble portrait busts of Prince William the Silent and his son, Prince Maurits, were done by Rombout Verhulst and were unearthed in the garden, where they were probably buried at the time of the French occupation. The entrance hall leads to the spacious Stucco Room, which rises the full height of the building. Yellow scagliola walls support a coffered ceiling executed by Carlo Castoldi.

After the death of King William II in 1849, Queen Anna lived in the house until her own death in 1865. Queen Emma, the mother of Queen Wilhelmina, spent her summers there after the death of her husband, King William III. Soestdijk was chosen by Queen Juliana as her permanent residence at the time of her marriage to Prince Bernhard in 1937. As a wedding present from the Dutch People, a part of the palace was modernized and some rooms were redecorated in the Art Deco style. Queen Juliana and Prince Bernhard continue to live in the palace today. In 1971, ownership of Soestdijk was once again transferred to the nation. The monumental prospect of the entrance façade, with its curving colonnades, can be seen from the road.

Soestdijk.
A detail of a porcelain dinner service that originally belonged to Queen Anna Paulowna.

Opposite page:
The Louvain room is named after one of the great battles fought by King William II. Portraits of this monarch and his wife by Jakob Joseph Eeckhout flank the white marble fireplace. The ormolu-mounted malachite furniture was brought from Russia by Queen Anna Paulowna at the time of her marriage in 1816.

GROENEVELD

Baarn, Province of Utrecht

Left:
A Rococo gable decorated with life-size mythological figures crowns the entrance façade.

The main building and its two symmetrical coach houses are completely surrounded by an ornamental moat.

Groeneveld is located on the edge of a large forest not far from the southern shore of the former Zuider Zee. A small house was built here around 1690 by Marc de Mamuchet, member of a Protestant family from Tournai who had fled north for religious reasons. In 1737, Groeneveld was inherited by Pieter Cornelis Hasselaer, an extraordinary man by all accounts. Hasselaer enlarged the house considerably, but financial difficulties forced him to sell it in 1754. He left for Indonesia to seek his fortune, returned a rich man twenty years later, and bought the house back. He became burgomaster of Amsterdam, but continued to spend time at Groeneveld with his wife and children until his death in 1797.

The house lies at the end of a long tree-lined avenue. The extraordinary concave brick façade has eleven bays of windows. The entrance, highlighted with stone, is capped with a Rococo gable that includes heraldic devices and two carved mythological figures, possibly executed by the sculptor Jan van Logteren. A white-painted balustrade runs the full length of the façade along the line of the roof.

The house is entered through a long corridor decorated with fanciful stuccos in the rococo style. These include a life-size figure of Neptune. All the rooms on the ground floor are arranged on either side of this central corridor. Groeneveld is now the property of the State Forestry Commission, under whose care the house and its large park have been completely restored. Groeneveld is open to the public all year.

KASTEEL DRAKENSTEYN

Lage Vuursche, Province of Utrecht

The story is told that when Queen Beatrix was a young girl, she was walking through the forest near her parents' house at Soestdijk, came upon Drakensteyn and immediately fell in love with it. Anyone visiting the house can see why. An ancient moated castle in the form of an octagonal jewel box, Drakensteyn is one of the most charming houses in the country.

The manor of Vuursche, which was given to the Bishop of Utrecht in 953 by the Emperor Otto, was united with the adjoining manor of Drakensteyn in 1571. Both were granted to Ernst van Reede by Prince Frederik Hendrik. In 1641, Van Reede pulled down the medieval fortified house, which had stood since 1362, and constructed the present building.

Drakensteyn passed through many hands before being bought from the Bosch van Drakensteyn family by Queen Beatrix, at that time Crown Princess of the Netherlands, in 1959. The princess undertook a complete restoration of the house under the guidance of the architect A. Verheus. Drakensteyn was her main residence from 1962 until 1980, when she became Queen and moved to Huis ten Bosch in The Hague.

Two long rectangular coach houses flank the large oval forecourt. The main house is not large and is built on an island surrounded by a shallow moat. The architecture is extremely simple, its most distinctive feature being the octagonal shape of the building. Seven sides of the octagon are painted white, and only the entrance side is faced in brick. The entrance door is surrounded by a stone portal with slender pilasters supporting a classical entablature and stone urns at the two ends.

The octagonal roof is surmounted by a balustrade and capped with a small decorative tower. It is from the tower that the Queen's standard is flown whenever she is in residence. Drakensteyn remains her private property and is not open to visitors.

Drakensteyn was given its octagonal shape in the seventeenth century.

SLOT ZUYLEN

Oud Zuilen, Province of Utrecht

Utrecht is one of the oldest settlements in the Netherlands. Founded by the Romans on the river Rhine, it remained an important city throughout the Middle Ages. The Bishops of Utrecht held the rank of Princes of the Holy Roman Empire, and ruled a large area of the country.

The name of Zuylen itself supposedly has a Roman origin, being either a corruption of the patronymic of the general Lucius Cornelius Sulla or the direct translation of the Italian word *colonne* into the Dutch *zuilen*. A member of the Roman princely family Colonna is known to have been in this area at the time of Charlemagne. Whatever their origin, the Zuylens were a very old family. Steven van Zuylen is mentioned in a document dating from 1278.

Van Zuylen was probably the builder of the simple fortified tower that already stood on this site in the thirteenth century. Strategically located on the river Vecht, which was the principal waterway connecting the Rhine to the Zuider Zee, the tower must have formed part of the defenses of the city of Utrecht, a short distance to the south.

The medieval castle was destroyed during the protracted civil war between the Hoeks and the Kabeljauws, which were opposing political factions for more than a century. Frank van Borselen, who was a leading Kabeljauw, inherited the ruins of the castle in 1422. He is the hero of the first of many romantic tales associated with Slot Zuylen. Having fallen in love with Jacoba van Beieren, one of his sworn enemies, he married her in secret. After their forbidden union was discovered, he was sentenced to death. However, she saved his life by renouncing both her property and her beliefs.

Slot Zuylen remained unused for many years. Between 1510 and 1528, it was rebuilt over the old ruins following an irregular quadrangular plan. The castle kept this appearance until the middle of the eighteenth century, by which time it must have seemed completely out of fashion. Baron Diederik Jacob van Tuyll van Serooskerken, whose grandfather had bought the property in 1665, decided to completely modernise the house. Van Tuyll had married an heiress from Amsterdam, Jacoba de Vicq. It is likely that his wife's considerable fortune encouraged him to engage an important architect for the project. The man chosen was Jacob Marot, who had learned his craft from his father, Daniel. The elder Marot, who was still alive, had been an influential figure in the world of Dutch architecture for more than sixty years and had carried out many commissions for the House of Orange.

Jacob Marot was asked to convert the rambling castle into a gracious

Zuylen.
The portrait of a seventeenth-century ancestress looks down with seeming disapproval on a charming doll's house. The inscription means "childhood joy."

Opposite page:
Jacob Marot created an entrance hall between an existing wall and a new one designed with numerous large windows to catch the southern light.

residence. However, the Van Tuylls never intended to tamper with the venerable appearance of the building, suggestive as it was of their family's antiquity. On the contrary, they must have been eager to maintain their social distance from the many *nouveaux riches* Amsterdam merchants who were busy building summer houses further down the river Vecht. The only important change that Marot made to the exterior of Slot Zuylen was to create a new entrance façade on the south front. He devised a spacious open forecourt by demolishing one wall of the former central courtyard and filling in the moat on that side. A large entrance hall was created between an existing wall and a new one designed by Marot with numerous large windows to catch the southern light. Many of Marot's drawings for the ambitious redecoration of the interiors are still in the house.

Isabelle van Tuyll van Serooskerken, known as Belle van Zuylen, was born in the castle in 1740. By all accounts, she was one of the most intelligent and fascinating women of her time. James Boswell, who met her in 1763 while studying in Utrecht, became besotted with her. "And yet just now a Utrecht lady's charms make my gay bosom beat with love's alarms," wrote the great diarist. She reportedly found him lovable but a bit strange.

Extraordinarily advanced in her thinking, Belle was among the very first writers to advocate the emancipation of women. Her rejection of social and moral conventions caused a mild uproar. She eventually married her brother's Swiss tutor and moved with him to Switzerland. Under her married name, Madame de Charrière, she continued her prolific literary production. She wrote essays, novels, and plays, and even composed

Zuylen.
Following pages, 116 and 117:
Belle van Zuylen's bedroom.

Following pages, 118 and 119:
The walls of the great room are
completely covered with
seventeenth-century verdure *tapestries.*

music. Her portrait was drawn by Maurice Quentin de Latour and sculpted by Jean Antoine Houdon. Copies of both works are displayed in her bedroom in Slot Zuylen.

The building has remained fundamentally unchanged since it was finished in 1753. A double staircase in the entrance hall leads to the *piano nobile*. The Delft tapestries that completely cover the walls of the Great Room were woven around 1643 in the workshop of Maximiliaan van der Gught. They depict imaginary landscapes behind a foreground of trees. The many delightful details include flowering plants and ornamental birds.

Portraits of nine generations of Van Tuylls hang in the dining room, starting with Pieter van Tuyll van Serooskerken, who died in 1492, and ending with Diederick Jacob, Belle van Zuylen's father, who remodelled the house in the eighteenth century. Slot Zuylen remained in the possession of the family until 1951, when a foundation was formed to look after its upkeep. The house is open to the public as a museum.

KASTEEL DE HAAR

Haarzuylens, Province of Utrecht

De Haar.
The reconstruction of the castle was directed by the architect P.J.H. Cuypers, whose designs show his extraordinary sensitivity to historical styles.

Bottom and far rigth:
The opulent decoration of the rooms includes a number of magnificent works of art.

Although the history of De Haar spans a period of seven hundred years, the present building was constructed at the end of the nineteenth century. Located in a low marshy area near the Old Rhine and very close to the city of Utrecht, the first castle was probably built on a higher strip of land, or *haar*, from which it took its name. Werner van de Haar is mentioned in 1282, and his grandson, Gijsbrecht Boekel van de Haar, is the first known occupant of a house on this spot. His granddaughter Josina, who inherited De Haar in 1440, was married to Dirk van Zuylen. The same family continues to occupy De Haar today.

The castle was destroyed in 1482 and subsequently rebuilt. By the end of the seventeenth century, however, it had already begun to deteriorate. By 1890, when it was inherited by Baron Etienne van Zuylen van Nyevelt, De Haar was a ruin. Although he and his wife, Baroness Hélène de Rothschild, lived in France, he decided to rebuild the family seat. With unrestricted funds at his disposal, he commissioned P.J.H. Cuypers, the most renowned Dutch architect of the day, to undertake the gigantic project. Construction started in 1892 and went on for fifteen years. The entire village of Haarzuylens had to be moved to make room for the garden.

The reconstructed castle is the largest in the Netherlands. The building, with its many turrets, makes a spectacular impression. Cuypers based his exterior plans on old drawings and prints of the medieval house,

but the monumental entrance front was entirely his creation. Built between two massive corner towers, it makes a fitting introduction to the house.

With nothing left of the original decoration, nor even old records to guide him, Cuypers freely recreated the interior of De Haar in an elegant and very personal version of the Neo-Gothic style. Like all great architects, Cuypers knew how to manipulate space. Directly after entering the house, the visitor comes into the central hall, created by building a roof over what had once been an open courtyard. The resulting space, which rises the full height of the building, is stupendously vast. The walls are lined with exuberantly carved decoration and surmounted by an elaborate ceiling. The central hall is one of the masterpieces of Dutch nineteenth-century domestic architecture. It is also a carefully contrived *coup de théâtre* which remains no less effective today than when the house had just been finished.

De Haar contains important collections of antique furniture, oriental porcelain, medieval sculpture, and some outstanding tapestries. But the greatness of the house lies in the tremendous variety of decorative details imaginatively designed by Cuypers and beautifully executed by his team of craftsmen. De Haar is open to the public except during the winter months.

HUIS DOORN

Doorn, Province of Utrecht

Huis Doorn, 20 kilometres southeast of Utrecht, lies in the middle of an old village in one of the most attractive wooded areas of the country. A fortified house was built on this site in 1322, but only after the destruction by fire of an even earlier building. In the seventeenth century, Huis Doorn belonged briefly to Prince Frederik Hendrik. Its appearance at that time was preserved in a drawing made by the artist Roeland Roghman. In 1780, the medieval house was pulled down and rebuilt in the neoclassical style. It passed through many different hands before being taken over by Baroness Heemstra at the beginning of the present century.

At the end of World War I, the defeated German Emperor, William II, was allowed by the Dutch government to settle in the Netherlands. The Emperor first stayed in Kasteel Amerongen as a guest of Count Bentinck. In 1919, he bought Huis Doorn. Very few structural changes were made before the Emperor moved in. The decoration, on the other hand, was carried out on a lavish scale. No less than sixty railway wagons were needed to transport the imperial possessions to Doorn. These included furniture, paintings, porcelain and carpets from the Hohenzollern palaces, as well as a dazzling collection of snuff-boxes formed by Frederick the Great of Prussia, which fortunately remain in the house. The Emperor lived here quietly until his death in 1941 at the age of 82. He is buried in a simple mausoleum on the estate.

Huis Doorn is marked by its massive gatehouse, built directly on the road in Dutch Renaissance style. The house is surrounded by a large park and is built in brick. The plain façade has projecting corner blocks and a pediment over the centre section. Huis Doorn is kept furnished as it was during the time of the Emperor's residence and is open to the public during the spring and summer months.

The neoclassical façade of Huis Doorn dates from 1780.

KASTEEL LUNENBURG

Nederlangbroek, Province of Utrecht

Lunenburg is located some 20 kilometres southeast of Utrecht in the geographical centre of the Netherlands. The nearest village is Nederlangbroek. Since a marsh was called *broek* in Old Dutch, the name of the village can be translated as "low long marsh." This area is indeed very marshy, and in the Middle Ages it was susceptible to floods from the nearby river Rhine. In the twelfth century, a canal was dug to help drain the land. Kasteel Lunenburg was part of a series of towers built along this canal in the middle of the thirteenth century. In 1340, when the castle was first mentioned, it was the property of Gerrit van Zijll.

Different owners made various additions to the medieval keep in the course of the years. In 1580, Lunenburg was sold to Godart Boll, who was mayor of Amersfoort. He added low buildings around a front courtyard and, by all accounts, turned the house into a pleasant country

Lunenburg.
An eighteenth-century polychrome plate is part of an important collection of delftware.

Top:
The architect E.A.Canneman succeeded in keeping the architecture of the new wing in harmony with the medieval tower.

residence. Lunenburg retained this appearance until the end of the nineteenth century, when Hendrik van Swinderen, who had inherited the property in 1860, transformed it completely.

Van Swinderen created a rectangular mansion of elegant proportions. The old tower was integrated into the new building and totally hidden under a layer of plaster. In 1883, Lunenburg was described as a ''fine stately place with proud lanes and ornamental ponds, a graceful iron gate and sturdy bridges.'' Lunenburg survived in this form until World War II, when it was occupied by German troops. Mistakenly believing that it was used to store military vehicles, the British bombed the house in 1943. Lunenburg was left in ruins.

In 1968, the property was acquired by a foundation based in Utrecht. The architect E.A.Canneman, whose work at Walenburg is discussed in a separate chapter, was asked to direct a complete restoration of the house. It was decided to do away with the additions built in the nineteenth century and to return Lunenburg to its earlier appearance. The restoration was completed in 1971.

The square brick tower, dating from the thirteenth century, stands alone on an island and is reached by means of a wooden bridge across the moat. The extremely thick walls and very small windows are reminders of Lunenburg's original defensive purpose. There is just one room on each of the four levels. The stairs are cleverly built within the thickness of the outside walls.

Romantic and picturesque as they may be, medieval towers are not practical places in which to live. Adequate living space for the new owners was provided in a totally separate house built beyond the moat on the northwest side of the tower. The design of this new house was based on various drawings made before Lunenburg was rebuilt in the nineteenth century. The use of traditional materials creates an amazingly successful harmony between the new elements and the original medieval tower.

Canneman's work at Kasteel Lunenburg shows his remarkable ability to interpret historical styles. His sensitive handling of scale makes the interiors of the house particularly attractive. The entrance leads directly to a central hall, which in turn opens onto the sitting room, library and dining room, all discreetly and tastefully furnished. A fine painting by Melchior d'Hondecoeter hangs above the dining room fireplace. Some outstanding pieces of antique Delftware grace the various rooms. Lunenburg is in use as a private residence. The imposing medieval tower can be seen quite clearly from the road.

Lunenburg.
Top:
*The painting over the dining room
fireplace is by Melchior D'Hondecoeter.*

*The long-case clock in the sitting room
is characteristically Dutch.*

129

KASTEEL WALENBURG

Langbroek, Province of Utrecht

Walenburg has become one of the most famous houses in the Netherlands. Combining the charm of a medieval castle with a garden of uncommon refinement and beauty, it attracts thousands of visitors every year. Until very recently, however, such acclaim would have been unthinkable. For many years, indeed throughout most of its long history, Walenburg was an uninhabitable ruin, and its garden did not exist.

The history of Walenburg begins in the middle of the thirteenth century, when the tower was built. Together with Lunenburg, its neighbour to the west, it was part of a group of protective towers constructed around the same time. Exactly what they were meant to protect remains a mystery, as Langbroek, the nearest village, never had any great strategic importance, and the surrounding marsh remained undrained and uncultivated until long after the towers were built.

The tower was raised to its present height around the year 1400, and in that form it stood alone until the middle of the sixteenth century. Someone at that time, having decided to live on the site, must have found the tower inconvenient as a dwelling. It was then that a wing was added on the south side. The size and shape of this addition have

Left:
The tower at Walenburg dates from the middle of the thirteenth century.

The house and the garden are linked by a wooden bridge.

131

Walenburg.
The thickness of the medieval walls can be seen most clearly around the window seats.

changed in the intervening four centuries, but tower and wing together still make up the present house.

More picturesque than beautiful, Walenburg changed hands many times until 1803, when it was bought by Baron Gijsbert van Lynden van Sandenburg. A period of benign neglect brought the house unchanged into the present century. By 1964, when Walenburg caught the attention of Mr. and Mrs. E. A. Canneman, the house had been vacant for a very long time. Mr. Canneman was an architect who specialized in historical restoration, and his wife was a noted garden designer. Together, they were uniquely qualified to bring Walenburg back to life.

The project took almost twenty years to complete. The structure of the tower was completely restored without the addition of any new elements. Mr. Canneman went to great lengths to preserve architectural details from the different building phases so that the tower would retain a full record of its history. The large room on the first level, directly over the vaulted cellar, was turned into a library. In keeping with the medieval character of the tower, the walls have been painted white.

The restoration of the wing was less restricted by historical considerations. The walls were taken down and rebuilt using old brick. The entrance was moved from the east side of the house, where it had been in former times, to the west. The small entrance hall immediately leads to the graceful sitting room. Three large windows open onto a wide terrace that runs the full length of the house. The eighteenth-century gray marble fireplace was found for the room. The beamed ceiling is partly of sixteenth-century origin.

The dining room is decorated with antique architectural elements successfully integrated into a harmonious unit. The display cabinet built into the south wall gives the room a characteristically Dutch appearance. The windows face the garden, planted by Mrs. Canneman on a separate island beyond the moat and reached by a wooden bridge built at the base of the tower.

The tower was used as the focus of a wide axial corridor lined with flower beds and crossed in the middle by a narrower secondary walk. This arrangement allowed Mrs. Canneman to create four separate gardens, each designed in a different style. The four quarters are kept separate by tall hedges of clipped yew.

After the death of the Cannemans, who had occupied the house on a lease, Walenburg returned to its owners, Count and Countess van Lynden van Sandenburg. Under the auspices of the Dutch Garden Foundation, the garden is open to the public several times every summer.

Walenburg.
Hunting trophies decorate the library.

KASTEEL AMERONGEN

Amerongen, Province of Utrecht

The village of Amerongen, some 25 kilometres east of Utrecht, is located on the banks of what is now known as the Old Rhine. For many centuries, and until the main flow of the current changed, this was the primary branch of the river, and therefore, the most important link between Germany and the North Sea. As early as 1286, a house was recorded on the site now occupied by Kasteel Amerongen. Nothing is known about the appearance of this early structure, but, being directly on the river, it was probably captured, destroyed and rebuilt many times before being bought by Goert van Reede in 1557.

In 1641, the house was inherited by Godard Adriaan van Reede, an important citizen of the Republic who served as ambassador to many foreign courts. In 1673, while Godard was in Berlin as envoy to the Elector of Brandenburg, the soldiers of Louis XIV captured the house

Left:
The upstairs gallery rises through the upper two levels of the house. The extraordinary series of ancestral portraits is unrivalled in the Netherlands.

Right:
A double bridge leads to the main entrance.

Following pages, 136 and 137:
The monumental fireplace in the great room is one of a pair decorated with portraits of the Elector of Brandenburg and his wife. The set of gilded chairs has been in the room since the eighteenth century.

Amerongen.
Right:
One of a pair of exquisite seventeenth-century cabinets which are kept in the great room. Their refined flower marquetry is attributed to Jan van Mekeren.

Left:
The tapestries in the tapestry room were kept in storage for many years. Their colours remain astonishingly fresh.

and burned it to the ground. Within weeks, Godard had started plans to rebuild. It has been suggested that Maurits Post, son of the celebrated architect Pieter Post, provided the new designs. However, considering that he was in Berlin at the time, it seems more likely that Godard sought advice from the Elector's Dutch architect, Mathier Smidt. The work was carried out by an Amsterdam carpenter and building contractor, Hendrik Gerritsz Schut, who, together with Godard's wife, Margaretha Turnor, very likely adapted the designs on the spot as the building progressed.

The Elector of Brandenburg graciously gave Godard 800 oaks for his building effort, and these were floated to Amerongen all the way from Berlin. Perhaps more practical was the gift of 40,000 guilders from the States General. But the house is large and economies were necessary. The extreme severity of the design is probably due more to financial than artistic reasons. Almost everything that could be salvaged from the old house was utilized in the reconstruction, and extravagant frills, such as carved ornamentation, were left out completely. Stone was used only to frame the main entrance to the house. Exterior work was finished by 1677.

Amerongen remained the property of the Van Reedes for more than three centuries. In 1879, the last member of the family died without issue and the property was inherited by a cousin, Count George Aldenburg Bentinck, who lived in the house until his own death in 1940, an extraordinarily long span. Bentinck devoted much time and effort to restoring Amerongen, and commissioned P.J.H. Cuypers, the renowned architect of the Rijksmuseum in Amsterdam, to remodel several rooms. At the end of World War I, Bentinck was asked by the Dutch government to lodge the defeated German Emperor, who had been granted asylum in Holland, for a period of six days. The Emperor and his retinue of forty-nine people ended up staying for a year and a half, which certainly must have made a dent in Bentinck's finances.

The house cannot be seen from the village, or indeed even from the entrance gate. The visitor must cross two bridges before catching the first glimpse of the impressive brick façade. Only the slight projection of the central section, which consists of three bays of windows, breaks the severity of the design. The sloping roof is capped by four massive chimneys. A remarkable two-level bridge leads to the main door. The principal feature of the entrance hall is its ceiling, painted in *grisaille* with vigorous scrolls and meant to suggest stucco. The coats of arms of Godard van Reede and Margaretha Turnor, builders of the house, are painted in the middle. Two niches in the whitewashed walls house marble busts of William and Mary. Of three large arches set into the west wall, the middle one holds a corridor leading to the Great Room. The two outer arches hold the first sections of the double staircase.

The Great Room faces the west and has an elaborate stucco ceiling. Two enormous marble fireplaces are topped by large portraits of Frederick William, Elector of Brandenburg, and his wife. The room contains a pair of cabinets with flower marquetry of extraordinary quality which were probably made around 1690 by the Amsterdam craftsman Jan van Meekeren. The large set of gilded Louis XVI armchairs was ordered from the Frenchman Jean-Baptiste Lelarge. Additional pieces in the same style were made in Holland. Next to the Great Room is the Tapestry Room, named after the set of wonderfully preserved Flemish tapestries that decorate the walls. Woven to the designs of the painter David Teniers, they retain their original colours in all their brightness. The room contains a French Louis XV desk where the last German Emperor, William II, signed his abdication on November 10, 1918, while he was a guest in the house.

The spectacular upstairs gallery, which rises through the two upper stories, is the showpiece of the house. It was designed by Cuypers to display the large collection of Van Reede and Bentinck family portraits and is topped by a vaulted ceiling elaborately painted. The room is now used regularly for concerts. Since 1977, Amerongen has been the property of the Stichting Utrechtse Kastelen and may be visited by the public.

Amerongen.
The dining room buffet is filled with Chinese porcelain. In the late nineteenth century, Count Bentinck commissioned the architect P.J.H. Cuypers to create the room out of the original state bedroom.

The West

MUIDERSLOT

Muiden, Province of North Holland

Until the opening of the Amsterdam-Rhine canal in the late nineteenth century, the river Vecht was the most direct water link between Utrecht and the great ports on the North Sea. In the whole of the Netherlands, and particularly in low-lying areas where the rain would often make road travel impossible, a boat was the only efficient means of transporting both people and goods. For political as well as economic reasons, it was vital to keep waterways open and navigable.

The impressive medieval fortress known as the Muiderslot is located at the mouth of the Vecht on the coast of the former Zuider Zee. Without understanding the strategic importance of the river, the presence here of such a formidable castle would seem illogical. Floris V, Count of Holland, constructed the first fortified house on this spot around 1285. An ambitious ruler, he had tried to unify a large territory under his control. In 1296, after being held prisoner in the Muiderslot, he was murdered by his enemies. The Muiderslot was later razed to the ground.

A new castle was built on the old foundations in 1370 and enlarged in 1386, at which time the building assumed the shape it has since retained. It played an important role at the time of the war against the Spanish. Robert Dudley, Earl of Leicester, lived in the Muiderslot during his unsuccessful tenure as governor of the Netherlands.

The most flourishing period of the castle's history started in 1609, when Pieter Corneliszoon Hooft took up residence in the Muiderslot. Hooft was the towering literary figure of the Dutch golden age. He combined the lofty humanism of the Italian Renaissance with the democratic ideals of his own native culture. Hooft's *Granida* was one of the most admired and influential Dutch plays of the seventeenth

The Muiderslot has retained its forbidding medieval appearance.

Muiderslot.

Top and opposite page:
The present structure dates from the
end of the fourteenth century. Modern
visitors are still required to cross the
drawbridge to enter the castle.

Following pages, 148 and 149:
The painted cradle at the foot of the
Dutch seventeenth-century bed lends a
domestic touch to the otherwise austere
bedroom. The portrait of the two
swaddled infants records their death in
April 1617.

century. In 1613, he wrote *Geeraerdt van Velsen*, a dramatised version of the murder of Count Floris V, the original builder of the Muiderslot. Hooft's monumental *History of the Netherlands* was published in twenty volumes in 1642. As a poet, dramatist, and historian, his prodigious output remains unequalled in the Dutch language.

The Muiderslot became a place where cultivated people could meet to exchange opinions and share new ideas. Hooft's friends included the poet Joost van den Vondel, the composer Jan Pieterszoon Sweelinck, and Constantijn Huygens, who was a poet and composer as well as the secretary of Prince Frederik Hendrik. This group of intellectuals, which eventually became known as the Muiderkring, gradually dissolved after Hooft's death in 1647. In 1954, the Muiderkring was revived in an attempt to keep alive the ideals of Hooft's time.

The Muiderslot was used alternately as a state prison and an ammunition warehouse during the eighteenth century. In 1825, it was in such bad condition that it came under threat of demolition. It was saved by King William I after a group of people, conscious of the Muiderslot's historical importance, appealed for his intervention. The restoration of the castle, which lasted until 1909, finally got under way in 1895. It was carried out under the supervision of the architect J.W.H. Berden. P.J.H. Cuypers, whose work at Kasteel De Haar is discussed in another chapter, gave sporadic advice.

The forbidding appearance of the building was determined by military rather than esthetic reasons. Impenetrable brick walls encircle the central courtyard. Massive round towers stand at the four corners. The wide moat is still crossed today by means of a drawbridge. The

147

medieval look of the exterior is not continued inside, where the various rooms have been arranged in the style of the seventeenth century. A portrait of Pieter Corneliszoon Hooft is displayed in the Great Hall. The floor is laid with black and white marble tiles. One wall is decorated with a large Flemish tapestry, dating from the seventeenth century, which depicts Alexander the Great and his wife, Roxane. A rare Dutch bronze statue of Hercules is displayed on the Renaissance oak sideboard.

The Muiderslot is the property of the Dutch State. After another restoration, undertaken between 1956 and 1972, the castle was opened to the public as a museum.

HUIS TE MANPAD

Heemstede, Province of North Holland

Surrounded by the flat sandy terrain that was so frequently pictured by Dutch landscape painters, Huis te Manpad was built in 1623 directly outside the village of Heemstede. Just four kilometres away is Haarlem, which at that time was the most important cultural centre in North Holland, far more so than Amsterdam, which eclipsed it only later in the seventeenth century.

The architecture of the house was not unusual. Compact and small, it was built in red brick and surrounded by a moat. In 1720, it was acquired by Wigbolt Slicher, who started to enlarge the building before his death two years later. The magnificent linden trees that stand in front of the house on either side of the axial drive were planted in 1721. Slicher's widow completed her husband's plans, but sold the property in 1730.

The garden front and the entrance façade.

Manpad.

The nineteenth-century tea pavilion is built on the banks of the ornamental lake.

Oposite page:
Massive stone statues are placed in the centre of the two ornamental pavilions.

Two wonderful stone statues are placed in the park directly behind the house. They are signed by the Dutch sculptor Jan van Logteren and dated 1734.

Following pages, 156 and 157:
The dining room walls are covered with paintings by Jurriaan Andriessen.

The two curving ornamental pavilions erected in 1742 make up the most prominent decorative feature of the house. Designed by the architect Adriaan Speelman to frame the wide forecourt, they are built around large red niches housing monumental stone figures. Unparalleled in the Netherlands, these two pavilions give Huis te Manpad an architectural grandeur infrequently found in a building its size.

The house is entered through a long corridor paved in white marble. At the very end is the dining room, added to the house in 1760 and decorated at that time with a magnificent series of pastoral scenes carried out by Jurriaan Andriessen, a painter from Amsterdam. The paintings depict imaginary Italian landscapes crowded with figures pictured around classical buildings. Similar scenes had been painted by Dutch artists since early in the seventeenth century, and Andriessen was one of the last exponents of this style. The dining room is furnished with a set of sixteen Dutch dining chairs dating from the mid-eighteenth century. The wind rose set over the fireplace is still in working order.

In 1953, Huis te Manpad was bought by a retired Dutch diplomat, Jan Visser, who had been ambassador to the Swedish court for many years. He devoted the rest of his life to the restoration and upkeep of the house and park. Huis te Manpad is still furnished the way it was when Mr. Visser was in residence. The small library, which overlooks the park, contains many mementos of Mr. Visser's diplomatic career.

The grounds are large and include a charming tea pavilion built on the lake. Two wonderful stone statues in the park directly behind the house are signed by the Dutch sculptor Jan van Logteren and dated 1734. The house can be seen very well from the road.

KASTEEL DUIVENVOORDE

Voorschoten, Province of South Holland

In Leiden's Lakenhal Museum there is a large tapestry made at the end of the sixteenth century to commemorate the heroic defense of the city in 1574, when it was besieged by Spanish troops. The city was saved only by opening the dikes, which caused a flood and allowed provisions and men to reach the population by boat. Kasteel Duivenvoorde is pictured in the tapestry, the earliest known representation of the building. The history of Duivenvoorde, however, begins in 1226, when it was mentioned for the first time. It was then the property of a Leiden family named Van Duivenvoirde.

Johan van Duivenvoirde, also called Johan van Wassenaer, inherited the castle in 1600. He had built a large house in The Hague, possibly following a design provided by Adriaen Fredericksz. When he turned his attention to the remodelling of his country seat, it is likely that Johan used the same architect. The building, completed in 1631, consisted of three sections arranged around a courtyard. Johan's grandson, Jacob van Wassenaer, inherited Duivenvoorde in 1681 and began to remodel both the house and the garden.

Jacob was succeeded by his son, Arent, who was a friend of William III. Arent had gone to England in 1689 and had married the daughter of the Earl of Portland, one of William's closest advisers. It was probably as a result of Arent's friendship with the King that Daniel Marot became involved in the remodelling of the great room, begun in 1702.

The rest of the eighteenth century was not a flourishing time for Duivenvoorde. Following Arent's death in 1721, the property passed to his daughter. By 1793, the contents of the house had been sold and the building itself was under threat of demolition. In 1817, ownership of Duivenvoorde again passed through the female line, this time to a girl barely ten years old. Amazingly, it is because of her that the house survived. At the age of 27, she married Baron Steengracht, son of the first director of the Royal Cabinet of Paintings in The Hague. The Steengrachts together restored the house and grounds. The formal garden, which dated from the late seventeenth century, was replaced with a landscaped park. In place of the former axial avenue, a winding road now approaches the house from the side.

The entrance front is dominated by three massive chimneys. The central block incorporates the thirteenth-century keep and is flanked by two projecting corner wings. The windows are surmounted by decorative arches in stone and brick dating from the 1631 rebuilding. The wide terrace, running the full length of the house, was constructed for the

Duivenvoorde.
The brick arches in the entrance hall date from the 1631 rebuilding. The large painting depicts Jan van Wassenaer, who died in 1544.

Steengrachts in 1845. Decorated with a group of superb stone vases salvaged from the earlier formal garden, the terrace conceals the medieval moat and gives Duivenvoorde the appearance of a romantic house built on an ornamental lake.

The entrance hall retains its painted ceiling from 1631. Stone fragments dating from Roman times and unearthed on the banks of the Rhine are built into the walls to remind the visitor of the antiquity of the site. Directly to the north is the great room, decorated in the early eighteenth century by Daniel Marot. Many of the drawings made for this project have survived and are still in the house. The plaster ceiling was probably executed by Gianbattista Luraghi, who is known to have worked with Marot at the Palace of Het Loo. Set over the red marble fireplace

Duivenvoorde.

The decoration of the great room was designed by Daniel Marot in the early eighteenth century.

is a painting of Johan van Wassenaer and his family done by Theodorus Netscher in 1702 and based on a Jan Mytens portrait of 1643, which is still preserved in the house. Set into the walls are a series of large paintings of four generations of van Wassenaers, all enlarged from earlier portraits.

Duivenvoorde has never been sold. Baroness Ludolphine Schimmelpenninck van der Oye, the last private owner, transferred the estate to a foundation to ensure the survival of the house and park. In 1963, following a complete restoration done under the supervision of the noted Dutch architect E.A. Canneman, the house was opened as a museum. The foundation regularly makes the great room available for concerts and private receptions. The house may be visited by the public during the summer months.

HUIS TEN BOSCH

The Hague, Province of South Holland

From The Hague, which for centuries has been the seat of the Dutch court, an ancient road leads northward to Leiden and borders on a wooded area known as the Forest of The Hague. Surprisingly, this area survives almost unchanged since the days of the stadholders. Even more surprisingly, the Huis ten Bosch, or House in the Forest, survives as well, barely visible from the road and still lived in by the descendants of the couple who built it more than three centuries ago.

Prince Frederik Hendrik was the third son of the great William the Silent. He became stadholder in 1625 and the same year married Amalia of Solms, a German countess who had arrived in The Hague as lady in waiting to the Winter Queen. Amalia and Frederik Hendrik were great art patrons and formed a very large collection of paintings which included not only several works by Rembrandt, but many others by major Flemish and Italian masters. Their building plans were no less ambitious. Even though his family had two large houses in The Hague, the Binnenhof and the Oude Hof, Frederik Hendrik started work on two major residences near the city. Amalia, however, wanted a summer house of her own, and in 1645 she was given a parcel of land for her use. Construction had already started by September of that year. The first stone was graciously laid by the Winter Queen.

The Winter Queen had been born an English princess and had married Frederick V, Elector Palatine. He was made King of Bohemia, but lost his crown after only one year. The brevity of his reign earned him the romantic epithet of the Winter King. He and the Winter Queen fled to Holland after their escape from Prague. Through his mother, the Winter King was a nephew of Frederik Hendrik, which assured his welcome in The Hague.

Gently projecting wings flank the central block of the palace.

Amalia showed great discrimination by selecting the architect Pieter Post to design her new house. Post, a painter as well as an architect, was one of the towering figures of the Dutch golden age. He had been partly responsible for the design of the Mauritshuis, which is one of the masterpieces of Dutch classicism. Built a few years earlier in the centre of The Hague, the Mauritshuis must have been familiar to Amalia, who clearly was inspired by its sober Italianizing style.

The compact building that Post designed for Amalia was constructed in red brick and crowned by an octagonal cupola. Fruit garlands carved in stone surrounded the windows on the entrance front. Initially, a portrait gallery had been planned in the central domed hall, which rose the full height of the building directly under the cupola. However, after the death of Frederik Hendrik in 1647, Amalia decided instead to dedicate this central hall to the memory of her dead husband. With time, the name of this room, which was known as the Oranjezaal, became the name of the house itself.

Although few visual records of the interior decoration have survived, the inventories of the time indicate that the house was luxuriously appointed. One painting, done for Amalia by the Flemish painter Daniel Seghers and originally displayed in the Huis ten Bosch, shows bunches of spring flowers set against an illusionistic background of swags and garlands carved around a stone niche. Derived from classical sources, decorative motifs like these must have been used a great deal in the interior decoration of the house.

From the time it was completed, the Huis ten Bosch became one of the great sights of The Hague, attracting many distinguished visitors from all parts of Europe. Two travellers from Bologna, the brothers Guido and Giulio de Bovio, came to see the house in 1677 and described it as "not large, but magnificent."

Amalia continued to spend her summers in the Huis ten Bosch until her death in 1675. In her will, the house was left equally to her four daughters and the children of the eldest. Amalia and Frederik Hendrik's only son, Prince William II, had died only three years after his father. His son, William III, took over the Huis ten Bosch in 1686, but never spent much time there, especially after he became King of England in 1689. When William III married his English cousin, Princess Mary, a sumptuous ball was held in the Oranjezaal.

In 1702, at the time of William III's death, ownership of the Huis ten Bosch passed to the King of Prussia, who was a grandson of Amalia and Frederik Hendrik. The house remained in Prussian hands until 1732, when it reverted to Prince William IV of Orange. William IV immediately started an extensive building programme to enlarge the Huis ten Bosch. The architect in charge was the celebrated Daniel Marot, who had started his association with the family of the Prince of Orange almost fifty years earlier. Under Marot's direction, the Huis ten Bosch was transformed from a small summer house into the grand Rococo mansion that we see today.

In the eighteenth century, life at the courts of Europe revolved a great deal around elaborately staged public functions. Marot's designs provided William IV with a setting for these formal occasions. He more than tripled the length of the façade simply by adding symmetrical wings on either side of the old house. These two wings, only one room deep

and built in the same red brick, project gently forward and create an effect both imposing and welcoming. Marot also designed a totally new entrance front and redecorated most of the interiors, which would have been considered old-fashioned by this time. To his eternal credit, he left the Oranjezaal alone, replacing only the fireplace. Although the principal part of the work was done by 1737, neither Marot nor William IV would live to see the project completed.

In 1734, following what had by then become a tradition with the men in his family, William IV married an English princess, Anne, eldest daughter of King George II. Anne served as Regent for her son, William V, who was only three years old when William IV died. Anne was extremely fond of music, and had studied with Händel before her marriage. Their correspondence shows that Anne frequently asked Händel to provide her with good singers for the many concerts that were organized in the Oranjezaal during her time.

No further changes to the house were made until after the marriage of William V to Princess Wilhelmina of Prussia in 1767. Following the French invasion of 1795, William V was forced to flee to England and was never to return. The Huis ten Bosch was confiscated and declared the property of the Dutch nation, as it is to this day. Most of the furniture was sold and many of the paintings were taken to France. At one point a hotel was being run in one of the wings, making the Huis ten Bosch surely the earliest stately home to take in paying guests.

In 1800, in an effort to protect the building, a few of the rooms were filled with assorted paintings and historical artifacts and opened to the public as a museum. Five years later, when the Republic was replaced by the Commonwealth, Rutger Jan Schimmelpenninck, Council Pensionary of Holland, seized the Huis ten Bosch. He removed most traces of the earlier occupants before being himself removed by Napoleon's brother Louis, who had been created King of Holland.

Louis and his beautiful Queen Hortense redecorated what was then called the Palais Royal du Bois in the most fashionable Empire style. In 1810, however, Holland was absorbed into the French Empire and Louis was forced to leave both the house and his throne. Napoleon's defeat was followed by the restoration of the House of Orange, and the Huis ten Bosch was returned to Prince William VI. In 1814, the year he was inaugurated Sovereign Prince of the Netherlands, William VI received the Czar of Russia in the Oranjezaal. One year later, the prince was confirmed as King William I by the Congress of Vienna.

The Huis ten Bosch was used regularly by the royal family during the rest of the nineteenth century. Queen Sophie, the first wife of King William III, was particularly fond of the house, and spent her final days there. In more recent times, Queen Wilhelmina also showed great affection for the Huis ten Bosch. A portrait of the Queen and her family in seventeenth-century costume was painted while they were living there.

The occupying German army took over the house during World War II, and at a certain point threatened to demolish it, but in the end it survived the war with only minor bomb damage. A thorough renovation was undertaken between 1950 and 1956, but Queen Juliana preferred to live in the Palace of Soestdijk. Another renovation, which lasted four years, was done for Queen Beatrix starting in 1977. She moved into the house after her ascension to the throne in 1980 and lives there now with her husband and three sons.

Huis ten Bosch.
Previous page, 165:
The walls and vaulted ceiling of the Oranjezaal are entirely covered with paintings. The largest is Jacob Jordaens' allegorical scene of Frederik Hendrik in victory.

Huis ten Bosch.
The extraordinary Chinese wallpaper in the Chinese room is intricately painted with figures.

Following pages, 168 and 169: The white dining room was designed by Daniel Marot in an exuberant Baroque style. The stucco work was carried out in the 1730's by Francesco Barberino.

The Huis ten Bosch was formerly approached from the forest, which allowed the visitor splendid views of Marot's elegant façade. The approach today is from the garden side, which unfortunately brings the visitor directly against the entrance front. Broad stone steps lead to four stone pilasters which separate the three bays. Topped by Ionic capitals, the pilasters originally supported the combined coats of arms of William IV and his wife, but these were removed at the time of the Commonwealth.

The entrance hall, spacious and light, is extremely plain. The white walls are hung with family portraits. Large display cabinets are filled with porcelain from a Chinese export dinner service presented to Prince William V and his wife and decorated with the arms of Holland and Prussia. The floor is laid with simple white marble tiles.

The austerity of the entrance hall does not hint at the opulence of the Oranjezaal directly behind it, which has remained basically unchanged since the house was built. Amalia commissioned some of the most illustrious Dutch and Flemish painters of the day to decorate this room. Jacob Jordaens was summoned from Antwerp to paint the scene of Frederik Hendrik in victory which covers one entire wall. Jordaens

shows the prince as a classical hero on a golden chariot, surrounded by a multitude of allegorical figures. This is the largest painting the Flemish master ever undertook. Even today, the vast expanse of the painted surface seems astonishing. Gerard van Honthorst was among those who painted the many other scenes from Frederik Hendrik's life which cover all the other walls.

Simulated Corinthian pilasters appear to hold up the profusely painted and gilded vaulted ceiling. A balustrated octagonal opening at the very top lies directly under the central cupola, itself resting on an octagonal drum set with eight large windows which allow the light to stream in. The octagonal motif is repeated in the pattern of the inlaid wooden floor. Pairs of carved and gilded wood wall-lights are set on the canted corners and match the four chandeliers. Four console tables dating from the eighteenth century and long banquettes upholstered in yellow silk damask make up all the furniture in the room.

The Oranjezaal is certainly a powerful memorial to the glory of Frederik Hendrik. But it was always meant to serve a purpose far more serious than simply indulging the whimsy of a proud widow. It must be kept in mind that the Dutch were still fighting for their independence at the time the Huis ten Bosch was built, and that Frederik Hendrik had played a very active role in that struggle. By paying homage to her dead husband, Amalia was also honouring the cause of Dutch independence. Seen in this context, the Oranjezaal becomes a very successful essay in political propaganda.

West of the Oranjezaal is the Japanese room, designed by Mathijs Horrix in 1791 as an audience room for William V. The walls were originally covered with Japanese silk elaborately embroidered and appliquéd with birds and flowers. It was so precious even in the eighteenth century that each panel was provided with a protective shade.

The decoration of the Chinese room, also done at the time of Prince William V, was planned to complement the extraordinary Chinese rice paper intricately painted with Chinese figures. The exceptionally beautiful stucco decoration on the ceiling shows playful Chinese figures and makes this room the richest example of the chinoiserie style in the Netherlands.

The white dining room lies in the west wing of the house. It was designed in an exuberant Baroque style by Daniel Marot for William IV. Ionic pilasters support the domed ceiling, which is embellished with uncommonly rich stucco decoration carried out by Francesco Barberino and incorporating both the crowned cipher of William and Anne and their combined coats of arms. A *grisaille* by Jacob de Wit over the fireplace is dated 1736 and represents the Four Seasons. Two other *grisailles* by de Wit date from 1749. Most of the rest of the west wing of the Huis ten Bosch has been set aside by Queen Beatrix to be used as guest quarters.

During the more than three hundred years since it was built, the Huis ten Bosch has served as a summer house, a hotel and a museum. It has been the residence, not only of twelve generations of princes of Orange, but also of kings and queens of England, Prussia and Holland. It has housed Nassaus and Bonapartes, Romanovs and Hohenzollerns. It has been used by republicans and monarchists alike, and has passed through Dutch, French, and German hands. A relic from the Dutch golden age, it is still vibrantly alive today.

HOFWIJCK

Voorburg, Province of South Holland

Left:
The house was probably designed by Constantijn Huygens, who was one of the most versatile men of the Dutch seventeenth century.

Top:
The main room of Hofwijck, which is now a museum dedicated to Huygens and his son Christiaan, who invented the pendulum clock.

Hofwijck is the creation of Constantijn Huygens, one of the most extraordinary Dutchmen of his time. He was a man of prodigious learning and multiple accomplishments, a scientist and poet as well as a composer. One of the leading intellectuals in the country, he served as private secretary to three successive Princes of Orange: Frederik Hendrik, William II, and the Stadholder-King William III. He counted many artists among his friends, including Jacob van Campen and Pieter Post, architects of the Mauritshuis. It is here that the large Adriaen Hanneman portrait of Huygens and his five children is now preserved. The painting depicts a man of fashion, an elegant and polished courtier.

One of Huygens' duties was to advise Frederik Hendrik on artistic matters. When the Prince commissioned a series of paintings from Rembrandt, he used Huygens as an intermediary. In a letter dated 1639, Rembrandt informed him that two of the pictures were ready and that he could deliver them to his house, "as happened before." Rembrandt ended the letter by saying that "because my lord has been troubled in these matters for the second time," he would also deliver a painting "ten feet long and eight feet high" as a present for him which he hoped would do honour to his house. It is tempting to speculate that Huygens brought the painting to Hofwijck, but he probably kept it in his house in town.

In 1636, Huygens bought a plot of land directly outside The Hague and had a small house built as a retreat. He named the property Hofwijck, which means "escape from the court." The house was probably designed by himself, although the plans must have been seen and approved by both Van Campen and Post. Very little remains of the large garden that originally surrounded the house. Encircled by a wide moat, the compact brick structure forms a double cube. Painted niches ornament the four façades.

Following Huygens' death in 1687, Hofwijck passed to his son, the celebrated scientist Christiaan Huygens, who spent his summers in the house until his own death in 1695. Christiaan is remembered in history as the inventor of the pendulum clock, but his contributions to the field of optics were even more impressive. He refined telescope lenses and was the first to discover one of the satellites as well as the rings of the planet Saturn. Many of his astronomical observations were made from the garden at Hofwijck.

In 1914, Hofwijck was acquired by the Huygens Society. Under their auspices, the house was restored and organized as a museum dedicated to Constantijn and Christiaan Huygens.

HET HUYS TEN DONCK

Ridderkerk, Province of South Holland

The first Dutch garden folly was built behind Het Huys ten Donk in 1775. The park was one of the first in the Netherlands to be laid out in the English landscape style.

Bottom:
The house seen from the garden.

Het Huys ten Donck sits peacefully on the flat alluvial landscape formed by the three great rivers that come together and empty into the North Sea at Rotterdam, just ten kilometres downstream. Somewhere near this spot there must have been a rise in the level of the land. *Donck* is an old Dutch word meaning mound or small hill, and so it is to this mound, no longer visible, that the house owes its name.

In an area of frequent floods, a mound provides natural protection against the tides and makes a favourable building site. A fortified farm already stood on this spot in the fifteenth century, and there are records of its sale in 1544. The house was captured by Spanish troops in 1575 and burned to the ground. It had been rebuilt by 1628, as in that year it was mentioned for the first time. In 1676, it was sold again, but the new owner died shortly after taking over and left the property to his

Het Huys ten Donck.
The staircase balusters are carved in the Rococo style.

Opposite page:
The entrance hall runs almost the full width of the house. The sleigh was a present from Queen Wilhelmina to the grandmother of the present owner, who was Mistress of the Robes to the Queen.

sister, who was the widow of Ulrich van Zoelen and a direct ancestress of the present owner. The house next passed to her son, and from him to his daughter, Catharina, who married Cornelis Groeninx in 1702. The next owner of the house was Otto, son of Catharina and Cornelis Groeninx. A man of great resourcefulness, Otto added his mother's name to his own, and since his father had bought the nearby lordship of Ridderkerk, he added that name as well, becoming Otto Groeninx van Zoelen van Ridderkerk.

It had become the fashion among Dutch merchants, grown enormously rich from trade, to build elaborate pleasure houses in the country. When Otto decided to build such a house for himself, he turned his attention to his parents' old house. It must have been the location that appealed to him: quite near to Rotterdam and directly on the river. Like their Venetian counterparts, the Dutch liked to build their pleasure houses along the water, where they could be reached fairly easily. Certainly nothing else about the old house could have been much to Otto's taste, for in 1746 he had it entirely pulled down. We can still get an idea of its appearance from two overdoor views in the dining room. Behind elegant figures attired in eighteenth-century dress, we can make out the step gables of a medieval moated house.

Otto's timing was extremely fortunate. In 1747, just one year after Otto started his new house, Prince William IV of Orange was finally ratified as Stadholder of the United Provinces, the office being declared hereditary in the prince's family. This was a tremendous stroke of luck for Otto, who had always been an unwavering supporter of the House of Orange. Grateful for his loyalty through the years, William named Otto to the post of burgomaster of Rotterdam. As one of the directors of the Dutch East India Company, Otto was one of the wealthiest citizens of Rotterdam, and it is likely that his new position added not only to his prestige, but also to his fortune. What is certain is that the decoration of the new house was considered so extravagant that Otto felt compelled to destroy all the bills.

Het Huys ten Donck was built to be used only for day visits. Otto would fill the house with his friends and business connections, but they would all return to Rotterdam in the evening. In fact, bedrooms were not even included in the original plan. Otto died in 1758, possibly before work on the house was completed, and his son Cornelis, who was only eighteen, became the new owner. Cornelis and his wife were very fond of entertaining, and their guest book, started in 1765, is still in the house. It contains many signatures of important Rotterdam politicians as well as foreign guests.

Het Huys ten Donck is built very close to the road, which gives the house the look of an urban rather than a country residence. There is no lawn in front, no stately walk bordered with trees to frame our view, but only a small gravel forecourt, and even this must be approached from the side and not down a central avenue. From this lack of a formal approach, as well as from the almost total absence of architectural ornament, it is clear that the intention of the anonymous architect was to downgrade the importance of the house. In this, Het Huys ten Donck is characteristic of the familiar Dutch preference for keeping a low profile. The visitor is given no clues to the opulence that lies inside.

The plain but elegant façade, built in red brick, is almost exactly

twice as wide as it is high. The only ornament is the wooden pediment, which is carved with the coats of arms of Jonkheer W.G. Groeninx van Zoelen and his wife, Baroness Rengers, parents of the present owner. The date 1746 is carved in the cornice directly below. Nine bays of windows are divided into three groups of three, with the central group projecting slightly forward. The windows on the *piano nobile* are quite tall, and are neatly aligned with those on the back. Light is a precious commodity in the north of Europe, and providing as much of it as possible has always been of primary importance to Dutch architects. The arrangement of the windows allows light to stream through the main rooms of Het Huys ten Donck to a degree unrivalled in any other Dutch house of its time.

The long entrance hall has a simple stone floor. Directly facing the entrance is a double door leading to the dining room, located within quick and easy reach of the kitchen. As logical as this arrangement might seem today, it was highly unusual at that time. Set above the dining room door, and almost the first thing that can be seen as the visitor enters the house, is a stucco allegory of the Dutch East India Company. It shows a woman with a cornucopia, which is always the symbol of prosperity, being pulled on the water by sea horses. The obvious purpose is to remind the visitor of Otto's position in the business world. To underline the point, bundles stamped with the monogram of the Dutch East India Company are shown on one side. This small stucco allegory, placed as it is directly inside the entrance door, is the visitor's introduction to Otto.

The walls on either side of the dining room door are set with interior windows, another most unusual feature. These allow the light to flow freely from two opposite directions. A stucco overdoor at the east end of the entrance hall shows a Dutch East Indiaman sailing past the Cape of Good Hope and a short French maxim: *si je vous perd, je suis perdu*, which means "if I lose you, I am lost." Shipping was a risky business in the eighteenth century, both for the sailors and their backers at home. Many ships disappeared at sea with their precious cargo, and fortunes were lost as suddenly as they were made. This kind of moralising allegory, meant to remind us of the impermanence of worldly pleasures, is typically Dutch.

The staircase has oak balusters carved in a vigorous Rococo style and brings us to the *piano nobile*. The view from the exceptionally large windows overlooks the dike and the river. The visitor can imagine Otto standing here to look out for the arrival of his guests. A gallery is built directly above the entrance hall and is decorated with a series of *grisaille* overdoors representing nine of the twelve labours of Hercules. They were done in the style of Jacob de Wit, possibly by one of his followers, but the artist's name is unknown.

The gallery leads to what is now called the smoking room, dominated by a large portrait of King William III of England at the Battle of the Boyne. The painting is one of two given to Otto by Prince William IV as a mark of his esteem, but it was probably placed here only in the late eighteenth century, when the decoration of the house was changed. Directly above the portrait, the stucco cornice is decorated with the coat of arms of William IV, which makes it likely that a portrait of that prince was originally displayed here.

In 1748, Otto had been a delegate at the signing of the Treaty of

Het Huys ten Donck.
The dining room was decorated in the neoclassical style in the late eighteenth century. The portrait over the fireplace, by the Flemish painter Nicolaas Delin, is dated 1777. It depicts the three children of Cornelis Groeninx van Zoelen, who inherited the house in 1758. The display cases hold a collection of Amstel porcelain.

Following page, 178:
The upstairs gallery. The overdoor painting is one of a series representing the labours of Hercules.

Following page, 179:
The Rococo decoration of the drawing room includes exquisite panelling and an elaborate stuccoed ceiling.

Aachen, and he considered this the highlight of his political career. A stucco allegory of the treaty, which brought an end to the War of the Austrian Succession, decorates the ceiling of the smoking room. It shows an angel pointing to heaven with one hand and holding an olive branch in the other, while next to him the torch of war is being extinguished by a cherub.

The splendidly appointed drawing room occupies the centre of the house and was clearly conceived as its showpiece. It still dazzles the visitor by its ample proportions and its lavish decoration. Separated from the gallery by a wall of interior windows, the room has panelling executed in a fully realized Rococo style, painted a light shade of gray and elaborately carved and gilded. The doors are similarly decorated and topped by *grisaille* overdoors in the style of Jacob de Wit. The stucco ceiling includes allegories of the Four Seasons carried out by two men from the Ticino, Carlo and Pietro Castoldi. Like many other Italian craftsmen of their time, the Castoldis travelled around Europe in search of commissions. Documents show that they started work in Het Huys ten Donck in 1756. All of the stucco work in the house was probably done by them.

Since its last sale in 1676, Het Huys ten Donck has changed hands only by marriage or inheritance. Starting in 1967, a thorough restoration of Het Huys ten Donck was undertaken by the present owner, who lives in the house with his family. A foundation has been set up to help with the maintenance of the house, and, under its management, the main rooms are occasionally made available for receptions and dinners. Otherwise, the house is not open to the public, but a splendid view of it can be had from the road.

The South

KASTEEL TER HOOGE

Koudekerke, Province of Zeeland

Zeeland occupies the southwestern corner of the Netherlands and is made up of a series of islands grouped around the estuary of the river Scheldt. Bordered by Belgium on the south and by the North Sea on the west, these islands have been made up over thousands of years by alluvial deposits carried here by the river. Middleburg is the capital, and Vlissingen (Flushing in English) the most important port.

Quite near both of these cities, and almost at the westermost tip of the country, is Kasteel Ter Hooge, built around 1300 by Anne van Borsselen. In the middle of the fifteenth century, Ter Hooge belonged to Louis of Bruges, Knight of the Golden Fleece and Stadholder of Holland and Zeeland, whose wife was a Van Borsselen. The castle was captured by Spanish soldiers in 1572, but was later returned to the family.

The present building was erected in 1755 after the old castle had been pulled down. The moat was filled in on the entrance side and turned into an ornamental pond behind the house. The entrance front was given a medieval appearance by the two high towers capped with spires. Ter Hooge changed hands various times, but it remained a family residence until 1950, when it was taken over by a nursing home. The house has now been divided and is occupied by four families.

The entrance façade is dominated by twin octagonal towers topped with spires.

KASTEEL MAURICK

Vught, Province of North Brabant

Kasteel Maurick is located on the outskirts of the village of Vught and borders on the main highway from 's-Hertogenbosch to Eindhoven, the two most important cities in the province of North Brabant. The beginnings of the castle date from early in the fourteenth century, when Jan Liescap and his son Gijsbrecht are known to have built a brick house with a tower on this site. The Liescaps were vassals of the Duke of Brabant, and Gijsbrecht fought with the Brabantine forces against the Duke of Gelderland. At the time of his death, the castle passed to Hendrik van Maurick. His widow moved into the castle in 1405 and gave it her husband's name.

In 1457, Maurick was sold to Goosen Heym. Possibly with the help of his son-in-law, Master Alard Duhamel, who was an architect, Heym began to enlarge the building. The Heym coat of arms can still be seen on the main façade. In 1601 and 1602, Prince Maurits of Orange commandeered Maurick, as did his brother, Prince Frederik Hendrik, during the siege of 's-Hertogenbosch in 1629. Jacqueline van Beresteyn, a widow, bought the castle in 1680. Her descendants lived at Maurick until 1884, when it was bought by Augustinus van Lanschot.

The castle is built entirely in brick and is surrounded by a moat. The curving entrance front, enlivened by two ornamental turrets, follows the line of the water. A drawbridge leads to the arched gateway, which is framed by a pair of round towers. The spacious open courtyard lies directly ahead. Kasteel Maurick is presently operated as a restaurant and can be visited by the public.

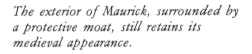

The exterior of Maurick, surrounded by a protective moat, still retains its medieval appearance.

KASTEEL HEEZE

Heeze, Province of North Brabant

The Dutch province of North Brabant occupies only part of the former Duchy of Brabant. For many centuries, this was one of the most prosperous and highly sophisticated regions of Europe. Today, Eindhoven is a major industrial centre. About 15 kilometres southeast of this city lie the village and castle of Heeze.

A seventeenth-century copy of a document dating from 1172, which is preserved in the archives of Kasteel Heeze, mentions a man named Herbertus and identifies him as lord of Heeze. A house on this location was chronicled in 1203, and although nothing is known about its appearance, it must have been spacious enough to hold a large number of the nobility of Brabant, Holland, and Cleves, who gathered here in 1318.

The medieval castle was called Eymerick. It stood on an island and

Heeze.
Top left:
Portraits of the present owner and his wife hang in the entrance hall.

Top right:
The neoclassical music room was created in the last years of the eighteenth century.

Opposite page:
The seventeenth-century Flemish tapestries in the drawing room depict scenes from the life of Alexander the Great.

had a somewhat haphazard square shape. In 1659, the property was sold for 201,000 guilders to a young nobleman, Albert Snouckaert van Schauburg. He had lost both his parents at a very early age and had been brought up in the cultivated circle of Constantijn Huygens, who was the secretary of the Prince of Orange.

It is certain that Snouckaert must have known the architect Pieter Post in The Hague. Huygens and Post were good friends and belonged to the same intellectual set. After the death of Jacob van Campen in 1657, Post was unquestionably the most important architect in the country. When Snouckaert decided to rebuild Eymerick, it was only logical that he should ask his illustrious acquaintance to provide the design. Starting in 1662, Post supplied numerous drawings for the remodelling of both the house and the garden. Many of these fascinating documents are preserved in the archives of Kasteel Heeze.

Post designed a large quadrangular building with square towers in the four corners to be constructed directly on the spot where the medieval castle stood. An immense forecourt was planned to the west, completely closed on three sides by coach houses and connected to the main building by a bridge. On entering the forecourt, the visitor would have been struck by the sight of the monumental façade lying at the end of the vast open space. Snouckaert must have liked the designs, for construction started without delay.

Unfortunately for the history of Dutch architecture, Post's extraordinary plans were not fully carried out. By the time Snouckaert died in 1678, only the buildings around the forecourt had been completed. In the early eighteenth century, stables were constructed on

Heeze.
Top:
Polished brass bed warmers hang next to a marble sink outside one of the bedrooms.

Top right and opposite page:
The bathroom is one of the first ever built in the Netherlands. It must have taken hours to fill the enormous black marble bathtub.

the east side of the forecourt, which Post had always intended should remain open. The medieval castle was left standing but unseen behind the stables, and work on the main house was never even started. Kasteel Heeze retains this shape today.

The estate changed hands various times during the eighteenth century. In 1733, it was bought by Baron François Adam de Holbach, who filled the house with beautiful furniture and luxurious works of art. In 1784, the property passed to Baron Jan Diederick van Tuyll van Serooskerken. Together with his young wife, Van Tuyll discarded much of the furniture as antiquated and remodelled some of the interiors in the most fashionable neoclassical style.

The Van Tuylls commissioned an architect from Liège, Nicolas Renier, to supervise the renovations. Renier created an exquisite oval music room directly over the main entrance to the castle. Fluted pilasters topped with Corinthian capitals support a vaulted ceiling decorated with musical trophies. All the elegant stucco work was designed by Renier in a pure neoclassical style and carried out by a fellow *Liègeois*, Lambert Jerna. Renier's preparatory drawings for the room are still preserved in the house.

Renier and Jerna were also responsible for the remarkable bathroom, one of the very earliest built in the Netherlands or indeed in all of

190

Heeze.
The blue bedroom retains its original neoclassical wallpaper from the end of the eighteenth century.

Opposite page:
The private sitting room of the present owners is filled with antique furniture and objects from the family's collection.

northern Europe. The decorative scheme here is appropriately based on the theme of water. Ionic pilasters flank rounded niches topped with shells and surmounted by dolphins delicately done in stucco. The spacious sunken bathtub is made of black marble. The floor is laid with black and grey marble tiles arranged in a decorative herringbone pattern.

The decoration of the large drawing room is dominated by a series of magnificent Flemish tapestries dating from the seventeenth century. They are built into the wood panelling and depict scenes from the life of Alexander the Great. The paintings grouped around the neoclassical fireplace include a portrait of Prince William the Silent. Kasteel Heeze has now become the property of a foundation, but it remains in use as a private residence by Baron Hendrik van Tuyll van Serooskerken and his family. Visitors are permitted to view some of the rooms during the summer months.

KASTEEL HILLENRAAD

Swalmen, Province of Limburg

Limburg is the southernmost province of the Netherlands. It is long and narrow, and is bounded by Germany on the east and by Belgium on the west and south. The river Meuse flows north through a tranquil landscape of gentle hills and small farms. Kasteel Hillenraad is located in the middle of a forested area near the banks of the Meuse. Less than ten kilometres south, at the point where the river Rur joins the Meuse, lies Roermond, an important trading centre during the Middle Ages.

Left:
The entrance to the formal garden is crowned by the coats of arms of Count Wolff Metternich and his wife.

Right:
Double flights of steps lead to the entrance of the castle. The pediment over the central section dates from 1620.

Hillenraad is mentioned for the first time at the end of the fourteenth century. In the course of the ensuing six hundred years, the property has never been sold, but has always been either inherited or acquired by marriage. It was enlarged and modernised at various times, notably in the seventeenth and eighteenth centuries, but the walls of the medieval structure have been retained in the entrance hall.

A long tree-lined avenue approaches Hillenraad from the west. A bridge over the moat leads to an arched gateway. Subsidiary buildings line the ample courtyard on three sides. These include a chapel as well as the usual coach houses. The fourth side of the courtyard is taken up by the large mass of the main house. Imposing and stately beyond its encircling moat, it is reached by way of a second bridge.

Hillenraad is built around a quadrangular central block dating from the earliest period of construction. Four square towers, capped by graceful spires, have been added at the corners. On the main façade, double flights of stone steps lead to a broad terrace in front of the entrance door. An ornamental pediment over the central section dates from 1620 and is decorated with the coats of arms of the Schenk van Nydeggen and D'Oyenbrugge families, who lived here at that time. The pediment was restored in 1767 after being damaged by a fire. It was then that the recumbent figures of Vulcan and Neptune, Roman gods of fire and water, were added, along with a Latin inscription, *Domine hinc fulgura quaeso repellas*, which roughly translated means "God please keep this house safe from fire."

A monumental double staircase dating from the eighteenth century completely dominates the entrance hall. The floor is laid diagonally with black and white marble tiles, and the plaster ceiling is decorated with delicate scrollwork. Directly behind the entrance hall is the ballroom, unchanged since its decoration in the eighteenth century and one of the most perfectly preserved interiors in the country.

The walls in the ballroom are decorated with Rococo wood panelling installed around 1750. The marble fireplace is surmounted by a mirror set into an elaborate stucco frame. The attention of the anonymous designer even extended to the window shutters, which are carved to match the general decorative scheme of the room. The magnificent parquetry floor is inlaid with an elaborate pattern designed to assist dancers in executing the steps of the minuet.

The decoration of the ballroom was commissioned by Countess Anna Catharina Schönborn, who was married to Count Willem Adriaan Hoensbroech and lived in Hillenraad. Their coats of arms can be seen over the entrance to the garden pavilion, which was built at this time. Their son, Philippus Damianus, was Bishop of Roermond at the end of the eighteenth century and lived in the house until the invading French army forced him to move out. Hillenraad remained empty and unused throughout the nineteenth century. After it was taken over by Count Hermann Joseph Ferdinand Wolff Metternich in 1909, the house underwent many necessary renovations.

There was much heavy fighting in the area around Roermond during World War II. Fortunately, Hillenraad suffered only minor damage, all of which has since been repaired. It is still in use as a private family residence.

Hillenraad.
Opposite page:
The entrance hall with its monumental double staircase.

Following page, 198:
The completely integrated decorative scheme of the ballroom includes the marble fireplace.

Following page, 199:
A large portrait of Count Wolff Metternich hangs in a sitting room.

KASTEEL VAALSBROEK

Vaals, Province of Limburg

Top:
The castle seen from the garden.

Bottom:
White coach houses stand on either side of the large forecourt. A double staircase leads to the main entrance.

Kasteel Vaalsbroek is located at the southeastern tip of the Netherlands, minutes away from both the Belgian and German borders. Aachen, the ancient capital of Emperor Charlemagne, lies only four kilometres to the east.

The castle was first mentioned in 1420, and it is known to have been rebuilt several times before becoming the property of Johann Arnold von Clermont in 1761. Clermont had moved to the Netherlands from Aachen for a combination of religious and business reasons. The house that he built in Vaals is now used as the city hall.

Vaalsbroek acquired its present form at this time. Clermont and his family used the house as a summer residence and had it enlarged and improved. The mausoleum, built in the park behind the house in 1788, is known to be the work of an architect from Aachen, Joseph Moretti. It is possible that Moretti was also involved with the rebuilding of the house. The spacious park was planted at the same time, but the original French design was replaced in the nineteenth century with the present English layout.

There are many hills in this area of the country, and they create a landscape that is not at all characteristically Dutch. Neither is the architecture of the house. There is no moat, and the outside walls are painted white. The central block is distinguished by the double set of steps leading to the main entrance door. The two lower side wings flank the large forecourt, which is closed in front by curving wrought-iron railings.

In 1974, Vaalsbroek became the property of the Foundation for Social Institutions in Heerlen. A complete restoration was carried out under the direction of the Maastricht architect J.H.A. Huysmans. The castle is now open to the public as a conference centre.

KASTEEL MHEER

Mheer, Province of Limburg

The round tower at Kasteel Mheer was probably built over Roman foundations constructed almost 2000 years ago, which makes it one of the oldest still-inhabited buildings in the Netherlands. In the nineteenth century, archaeologists found evidence of an even earlier prehistoric settlement indicating that the site was already occupied in the tenth century B.C. Roman pottery shards were unearthed in the courtyard of the castle in 1918, but, unfortunately, they were stolen from the house during World War II.

Limburg is rich in Roman remains. The provincial capital, Maastricht, which lies fifteen kilometres north of Mheer, was founded by the Romans at the spot where they could ford the river Meuse. The small Roman settlement at Mheer continued to be occupied during the early Middle Ages. The building is mentioned at the beginning of the eleventh century during the reign of the Emperor Henry II. It was one of the fortified castles that protected the border between the Duchy of Limburg and the Principality of Liège.

In spite of its long history, there is no record of Kasteel Mheer ever having been sold. In 1498, the property passed to a woman, Berbe ab Mere. Her greatgrandson, Jan Adolph van Ymstenroy, rebuilt the castle in 1612. After the death of his widow, Kasteel Mheer passed to her brother, Degenhard de Löe. One of his descendants, also named Degenhard de Löe, lives in the castle today.

The park around Kasteel Mheer is surrounded by an impressive brick wall, which is almost the first thing the visitor sees on arriving in the village. The approach to the castle lies behind the village church, which nearly hides the large brick and stone gateway. Dating from 1612, the

The striking façade was given its present appearance at the end of the nineteenth century.

Mheer.
This massive cupboard is characteristic of Dutch furniture from the seventeenth century.

Opposite page:
A child's sleigh casually occupies a niche in the formal entrance hall, which is decorated in the Empire style.

gateway is built around a rusticated stone arch and capped by a beautifully proportioned Renaissance scroll gable. The spacious inner courtyard is enclosed on three sides by long buildings. The castle, built at the western end of the courtyard, acquired its present look at the end of the nineteenth century. Many of the interiors were redecorated at the same time. Limburg is the only area of the country where quarries can be found, and stone is used quite generously in the construction. The castle is built around an open quadrangle that contains a long flight of stone stairs leading to the *piano nobile*. The stairs were changed at the time of the nineteenth century renovation, but there are plans to restore them to their earlier appearance. After twenty centuries of change, Kasteel Mheer has still not attained it final form.

Bibliography

ASLET, Clive. «Het Huys ten Donck, Ridderkerk.» *Country Life,* August 20 and 27, 1981.

ASLET, Clive, and Heimerick TROMP. «Kasteel Cannenburch, Near Apeldoorn.» *Country Life,* August 22, 1985.

ASLET, Clive. «Kasteel Keppel, Gelderland.» *Country Life,* August 25 and September 1, 1983.

BASTIAANSE, R., and H. BOTS. *Glorious Revolution: The World of William and Mary.* The Hague, SDU Uitgeverij, 1988.

BOOM, Florence Hopper. «Formality Enclosed by Water. The Gardens of Weldam Castle, Overijssel.» *Country Life,* August 26, 1976.

BRAASEM, W.A. *Een Rebelle aan de Vecht, Slot Zuylen en Zijn Bewoners.* The Hague: Esso Museumreeks, 1984.

BRAASEM, W.A. *Het Huis te Amerongen.* The Hague: Esso Museumreeks, 1981.

CANNEMAN, E.A., and Hans NIEUWENHUIS. *Kasteel Duivendoorde.* Doorn: Nederlandse Kastelen Stichting, 1987.

CANNEMAN, E.A. *Walenburg, Huis en Hof.* Amsterdam: Nederlandse Tuinenstichting.

CLEVERENS, R.W.A.M. *Het Huis Twickel en Zijn Bewoners.* Alphen aan den Rijn: Repro-Holland, 1981.

The Cooper-Hewitt Museum. *Courts and Colonies: The William and Mary Style in Holland, England and America.* Exhibition catalogue. New York: The Cooper-Hewitt Museum, 1988.

CORNFORTH, John. «Kasteel Amerongen, Holland.» *Country Life,* August 23 and 30, 1979.

DROSSAERS. S.W.A., and Th.H.LUNSINGH SCHEURLEER. *Inventarissen van de Inboedels in de Verblijven van de Oranjes 1567-1795.* The Hague: Martinus Nijhoff, 1974.

DUNNING, Albert. *Count Unico Wilhelm van Wassenaer: A Master Unmasked or the Pergolesi-Ricciotti Puzzle Solved.* Buren: Frits Knuf, 1980.

VAN DER FELTZ, A. C. A. W. *Kunstnijverheid Hannema-De Stuers Fundatie.* Zwolle: Uitgeverij Waanders, 1980.

GATACRE, E. V. «Variety of Vistas in Gelderland.» *Country Life,* August 25, 1977.

GROENINX VAN ZOELEN VAN RIDDERKERK, W. G. «Het Huys ten Donck.» *Country Life.* February 12, 1938.

Groninger Museum. *Allert Meijer, Schrijnwerker, Stadsbouwmeester; Jan de Rijk, Beeldhouwer.* Exhibition catalogue. Groningen: Groninger Museum, 1978.

HANNEMA, Dirk. *Flitsen uit Mijn Leven als Verzamelaar en Museumdirecteur.* Rotterdam: Ad. Donker, 1973.

HANNEMA, Dirk. *Verzameling Stichting Hannema-De Stuers.* Rotterdam: Ad. Donker. 1967.

HARRIS, Walter. *A Description of the King's Royal Palace and Garden at Loo.* London, 1699.

TEN HOEVE, S. *Epemastate en de Kerk te Ysbrechtum.* Leeuwarden: Stichting Monument van de Maand, 1989.

HIJMERSMA, Herbert Jan, and John CORNFORTH. «Kasteel Duivenvoorde, Holland.» *Country Life,* January 24 and 31, 1974.

JANSSEN, H.L., and Hans NIEUWENHUIS. *Kasteel De Haar.* Doorn: Nederlandse Kastelen Stichting, 1986.

JONGSMA, H. *Kasteelen, Buitenplaatsen, Tuinen en Parken van Nederland.* Amsterdam: Scheltema en Holkema's Boekhandel, 1912.

VAN DE KAA, Romke. *De Wiersse.* Vorden: Stichting Victor de Stuers, 1990.

KALKWIEK, K.A., and A.I.J.M.SCHELLART. *Atlas van de Nederlandse Kastelen.* Amsterdam: Sijthoff, 1980.

KAMERLINGH ONNES, G.A., and U.M. MEHRTENS. *Kasteel Vosbergen ter Heerde.* Zeist: Rijksdienst voor de Monumentenzorg, 1985.

KOOT, Ton. *Dat Was te Muden.* Amsterdam: Meijer Pers, 1976.

KOOT, Ton. *Het Mysterie van Muiden.* The Hague: Uitgeverij Nijgh & Van Ditmar, 1977.

KRANENBURG-VOS, A.C. *Het Loo*. Amersfoort: Uitgeverij Bekking, 1986.

TER KUILE, E.H. *Kastelen en Adellijke Huizen*. Amsterdam: Uitgeverij Contact, 1954.

LOONSTRA, Marten. *Het Koninklijk Paleis Huis ten Bosch Historisch Gezien*. Zutphen: De Walburg Pers, 1985.

National Gallery of Art. *Gods, Saints & Heroes: Dutch Painting in the Age of Rembrandt*. Washington: National Gallery of Art, 1980.

ORTENBURG-BENTINCK, Isabelle, and N.W. CONIJN. *Kasteel Middachten*. De Steeg: Kasteel Middachten, 1986.

VAN OIRSCHOT, Anton. *Het Kasteel van Heeze*. Doorn: Nederlandse Kastelen Stichting, 1985.

VAN OIRSCHOT, Anton. «De Kastelen in Zeeland.» *Monumenten Jaargang* nr. 9, 1988.

The Pierpont Morgan Library. *William & Mary and Their House*. Exhibition catalogue. New York: The Pierpont Morgan Library, 1979.

VAN RAAI, Stefan, and Paul SPIES. *In het Gevolg van Willem III en Mary*. Amsterdam: De Bataafsche Leeuw, 1988.

DE REGT, Evelyn. *Mauritshuis*. The Hague: Staatsuitgeverij, 1987.

ROSENBERG, Jacob, Seymour SLIVE, and E. H. TER KUILE. *Dutch Art and Architecture 1600-1800*. The Pelican History Art, third edition. Harmondsworth, Middlesex: Penguin Books, 1977.

SCHAMA, Simon. *The Embarrassment of Riches*. London: Collins, 1987.

SCHELLART, A.I.J.M. *Drakestein*. Amsterdam: AO Reeks, 1962.

SCHELLART, A.I.J.M. *Kastelen*. Deventer: Uitgeverij Ankh-Hermes, 1974.

SCHELLART, A.I.J.M. *Historische Landhuizen*. Deventer: Uitgeverij Ankh-Hermes, 1975.

Slot Zuylen. *Belle van Zuylen-Isabelle de Charrière*. Exhibition catalogue. Maarssen: Slot Zuylen, 1974.

TENGBERGEN, Annet. *De Acht Kastelen van Vorden*. Zutphen: De Walburg Pers, 1988.

THORNTON, Peter. *Seventeenth-Century Interior Decoration in England, France and Holland*. New Haven and London: Yale University Press, 1978.

TROMP, Heimerick, and B. ZIJLSTRA. *Kasteel Amerongen*. Doorn: Nederlandse Kastelen Stichting, 1985.

TROMP, Heimerick. «Heeze». *De Woonstede door de Eeuwen Heen* nr. 82, 1989.

TROMP, Heimerick. *Kastelen Langs de Wetering*. Zeist: Drukkerij Kerckebosch, 1968.

TROMP, Heimerick. *Kastelen Langs de Wetering II*. Zeist: Drukkerij Kerckebosch, 1971.

TROMP, Heimerick. *Kastelen Langs de Wetering III*. Zeist: Drukkerij Kerckebosch, 1972.

TROMP, Heimerick. *Het Koninklijk Paleis Soestdijk Historisch Gezien*. Zutphen: De Walburg Pers, 1987.

TROMP, Heimerick. *Kijk op Kastelen*. Amsterdam and Brussels: Elsevier, 1979.

TROMP, Heimerick. «Slot Zuylen.» *De Woonstede door de Eeuwen Heen* nr. 47, 1980.

TROMP, Heimerick. «Van Spaen, Piranesi en de zaal op Biljoen.» *De Woonstede door de Eeuwen Heen* nr. 65, 1985.

VAN DER VALK BOUMAN, J.M. *'T Konings Loo: Van Prinselijk Ontwerp tot Koninklijk Paleis*. The Hague: Esso Museumreeks, 1985.

VELDMAN, Freerk J., and Lieke VELDMAN-PLANTEN. *De Menkemaborg*. Doorn: Nederlandse Kastelen Stichting, 1984.

WAGENAAR HUMMELINCK, M.G. *Groeneveld*. Doorn: Nederlandse Kastelen Stichting, 1983.

CHRONOLOGY OF SUCCESSION

1559-1584 Stadholder Willem I, Prince of Orange.

1584-1625 Stadholder Maurits, Prince of Orange.

1625-1647 Stadholder Frederik Hendrik, Prince of Orange.

1647-1650 Stadholder Willem II, Prince of Orange.

1650-1672 The Netherlands controlled by the States-General.

1672-1702 Stadholder Willem III, Prince of Orange, King William III of Great Britain and Ireland.

1702-1747 The Netherlands controlled by the States-General.

1747-1751 Stadholder Willem IV, Prince of Orange.

1751-1795 Stadholder Willem V, Prince of Orange.

1795-1813 The Netherlands controlled by France.

1813-1840 King Willem I of the Netherlands, Grand Duke of Luxembourg, Prince of Orange.

1840-1849 King Willem II of the Netherlands, Grand Duke of Luxembourg, Prince of Orange.

1849-1890 King Willem III of the Netherlands, Grand Duke of Luxembourg, Prince of Orange.

1890-1948 Queen Wilhelmina, Princess of Orange-Nassau.

1948-1980 Queen Juliana, Princess of Orange-Nassau.

1980-   Queen Beatrix, Princess of Orange-Nassau.